MISSOURI HOMESTEAD

BOOK 1

MISSOURI HOMESTEAD

T. L. TEDROW

THOMAS NELSON PUBLISHERS
Nashville

Published in Nashville, Tennessee, by Thomas Nelson, Inc., and distributed in Canada by Lawson Falle, Ltd., Cambridge, Ontario.

While this book is a fictional account of Laura Ingalls Wilder's exploits, it retains the historical integrity of her columns, diary, family background, personal beliefs, and the general history of the times in which she lived. However, any references to specific events, real people, or real places are intended only to give the fiction a setting in historical reality. Names, characters, and incidents are either the product of the author's imagination or are used fictitiously, and their resemblance, if any, to real persons, living or dead, is purely coincidental.

Library of Congress Cataloging-in-publication Data

Tedrow, Thomas L.
    Missouri homestead / by T.L. Tedrow.
      (The Days of Laura Ingalls Wilder ; bk. 1)
    ISBN 08407399301
    1. Wilder, Laura Ingalls, 1867-1957—Fiction. I. Title.
  II. Series : Tedrow, Thomas L. Days of Laura Ingalls Wilder; bk. 1.
PS3570.E33M5 1992
813'.54—dc20
                                   91-46211
                                       CIP
                                       r92

Dedicated To

*Sam Moore, who has shown me that faith and
determination can move mountains.*

And Special Thanks To

*Carla: my wife, best friend, and coauthor.
When the chips were down, she picked them up and
we started again.*

*My four children, C. T., Tyler, Tara, and Travis,
who inspire and help with what I write.*

*My mother, Gertrude Tedrow, who
taught me faith, courage, kindness, love, and understanding.*

*My late father, Richard Tedrow, who told me I could be
anything I wanted. I miss him every day.*

*My sister, Carol Newman, and brother, Richard Tedrow,
who helped me through the hard times.*

CONTENTS

FOREWORD

Laura Ingalls Wilder is known and loved for her pioneer books and the heartwarming television series based on them. Though much has been written about the old West, it was Laura Ingalls Wilder who brought the frontier to life for millions of young readers.

The American West offered a fresh start to anyone brave enough to face the challenges. These people tamed the frontier, crossing the prairie in wagons carrying furniture, seeds, and children, looking for a place to build a new life. They went west to raise families, build farms and towns, churches and businesses. They went knowing they would face hardship and danger, but that those who survived could build a future for their children.

Laura Ingalls's adventures did not stop after she married Almanzo Wilder. She went on to become a pioneer journalist in Mansfield, Missouri, where for sixteen years she was a columnist for the weekly paper, *Missouri Ruralist*.

Laura Ingalls Wilder, a self-taught journalist, always spoke her mind. She worked for women's rights, lamented the consequences of war, and observed the march of progress as cars, planes, radios, and new inventions changed America forever.

While this book is a fictional account of Laura's exploits, it retains the historical integrity of her columns, diary, family background, personal beliefs, and the general history of the times in which she lived. However, any references to specific events, real people, or real places are intended only to give the fiction a setting in historical reality. Names, characters, and incidents are either the product of my imagination or are used fictitiously, and their resemblance, if any, to real-life counterparts is purely coincidental.

T. L. TEDROW

CHAPTER 1

ON THE ROAD TO MISSOURI

AUGUST 30, 1894

As the covered wagon splashed into a water-filled hole near the crest of a hill outside Springfield, Missouri, Laura's pencil slipped off the nickel notepad diary she was keeping. Other scratches on the pad testified to the rough road they'd been traveling.

Laura looked over at her husband. "Manly, can't you keep this wagon on the road? Look what you've done!"

Manly, rolling his eyes, barely looked at his pretty-but-plain twenty-seven-year-old pioneer wife. Manly's love for this bouncy, outspoken, impulsive woman was easy to see.

They were each other's best friends in a world of strangers and friends left behind. Though they loved each other fiercely, both were strong willed and enjoyed their playful teasing and arguing.

"Laura, if you'd look around you'd notice that these roads are filled with immigrants." Manly waved his hands as if addressing a convention. "Why, just look at them all. By jinks, this road looks like a city on wheels."

Laura put down her pad and looked around. Their seven-year-old daughter, Rose, who was holding Jack, the spotted bulldog, on her lap behind the wagon seat, peeked between Laura and Manly.

"Momma, why do all these people look so different?" Rose asked.

Laura, noticing how they dressed differently and hearing the strange languages of the families who greeted them, waved to a Frenchman, who tipped his hat without losing the beat of the song he was singing to his children.

"Rose, these people are from all over the world," Laura replied.

"Seems like the whole world is here," Manly commented.

Laura chuckled. "Oh, Manly, these people are doing what we're doing—hoping for a better life, leaving their problems behind."

Manly mumbled to himself, "If their behinds had stayed behind with their problems, we'd all be better off."

Laura sighed. "Manly, don't you know what it says on the Statue of Liberty that France gave us? 'Give me your tired, your poor, your huddled masses yearning to breathe free. Send these, the homeless, tempest-tossed to me; I lift my lamp beside the golden door!' "

Spurring on the team, Manly looked at Laura and said, "We got enough tired, poor, and homeless people here already. Ain't nobody lifting a lamp to a golden door for us."

Laura grabbed the reins and guided the team left, just missing another wagon. The driver let loose with a shaking fist and a string of Italian-American words that Laura hoped Rose didn't understand.

Handing Manly the reins, she said, "You better watch where you're going."

Manly shook his fist over his shoulder at the immigrant they'd just missed.

Laura looked at her husband with exasperation. "Manly, have you forgotten how we all got here in the first place?"

Manly snorted his disagreement. "Times have changed, Laura. Times have changed."

Like many Americans at the end of the nineteenth century, Manly thought America was getting too crowded. Millions of immigrants were headed to America. With strong, willing backs and a hunger to be free, they yearned to live in a country where people had the right to choose their own leaders and a chance to make their own fortunes.

America's prairie land was a welcome mat to the world, open land as far as the eye could see. On this ocean of glory, any sodbuster could claim a section of land as his own. The land-grant system and the desire of the railroads to settle customers along their lines had literally opened up the heartland of America.

Manly knew his family had arrived in America only a generation before, but like human beings everywhere, he was somewhat afraid of newcomers. He'd been born in America, and as far as he was concerned, his roots were in New York State, not in the land of his parents' birth.

Rose tugged at her mother's dress. "Where do they come from, Momma?"

Laura straightened the braids in Rose's hair and smoothed her dress. Jack yipped, and she scratched his head.

"Where do they come from? Why, they've come from everywhere on earth. The newspaper said that millions of people are coming to America looking for work. They're coming from Italy, England, Scotland, Germany, Poland, Ireland, Hungary, Russia, Norway, and . . ."

Manly "giddiyapped" the horses a little too quickly, jolting them back in their seats. "Excuse me for interrupting the class, but how can you tell the difference in all these folks?"

Laura shook her head. "I just look and listen. That man who just passed us was from France. I could tell by the language. 'Bonjour' is hello in French."

"And where'd you learn how Frenchies speak?" Manly asked, eyeing an approaching wagon.

Laura gave Jack a piece of beef jerky from the sack under the seat. "When we crossed the river, I heard one of the riverboat captains speaking that beautiful language. I asked him what he was speaking and where he was from. He was from Paris—Paris, France. Can you imagine that?"

Manly grabbed a piece of beef jerky for himself. "I imagine it would seem a whole lot better if they were still there."

As the horses began another uphill pull, Manly coached them forward. People seemed to be everywhere, their cows, goats, sheep, and children trailing behind their wagons.

Manly shook his head and turned back to his wife. "Where's that one from?"

Laura listened to the family talking and heard the distinctive Scottish brogue. It brought back family memories. "Scotland."

"Scotland! How do you know?" Manly exclaimed, slapping his hat. "They ain't wearing those kilt dresses!"

"I heard it in their voices. My great-great-grandfather was Johnnie Blue, from the Scottish peninsula of Kintyre," Laura said matter-of-factly.

"Never saw your pa wearing no kilt!" Manly joked.

Laura looked straight at him. "Manly, you old fool, when you come to America you leave a lot of the old country behind so you can become part of the new country."

Manly eyed her right back, trying to keep a straight face. "Those Scots we just passed were probably your cousins. I bet you had some secret hand sign that I didn't catch. That's how you knew 'em, isn't it?"

Laura, not catching the gleam in his eye, said, "If you'd talk less and listen more, most of your questions would answer themselves. You've heard a Scottish brogue before."

Manly took off his hat and wiped his brow. As another wagon came around the bend, he asked, "Okay, schoolmarm. Where be these people from?"

As they got closer, Laura saw that it was a family of black farmers heading back from town with a load of seed. "They're from Africa. They might not have come here by choice, but all the same, they're from Africa."

Manly scratched his chin. "I guess that one was too easy."

The family waved to the Wilders. Manly tipped his hat and Laura waved back.

Rose peeked under the edge of the wagon flap and saw a black boy about her age peeking back. She dropped the flap and turned to her mother. "Were they happy as slaves, Momma? That old farmer who camped beside us last night said people like that were happiest when they were slaves."

Laura looked at Rose. "Would you be happy to be held against your will? People are people, Rose. They all have the same needs to eat, sleep, have a roof over their heads, and be happy."

Manly "giddiyapped" the horses again. "Laura, you'd think you was givin' a sermon. Let's get back to the game of guessing where all these people are from." Looking at the wagon coming down the next rise, he said, "How about that one?"

Laura looked over, recognized the Russian flag flying from the wagon hoop, and said, "Russia."

"How can you tell?"

"I recognize the flag." Laura waved to the Russians and shouted, "Where're you heading?"

The man, dressed in a mixture of prairie and cossack clothes, smiled and said in broken English, "Biz-mark, Nor' Da-ko-ta."

"Good luck," Laura shouted, watching the Russian family heading toward the place she and Manly had just left. "You'll need it," she whispered. Just the mention of the Dakotas brought a wave of sad memories to her.

"Don't wish nothin' on 'em that we went through," Manly said, looking over at Laura, who was deep in thought.

Manly moved the wagon over to avoid another hole in the road. He wanted to get Laura out of her mood, so he playfully jabbed a finger into her side. "Okay, Miss Smarty-pants, let's find a wagon without no flag and see if you can tell me where it's from."

Laura shook off the memories and smiled bravely. "Just point one out."

Spotting one he thought looked right for stumping Laura, Manly pointed to a wagon parked against a growth of trees beside the road. "Where's that one from?"

Laura looked and looked and looked. Manly had stumped her! She hated to admit it, but he had.

As they passed slowly by the wagon, Manly smiled smugly. "Ha-ha. Got you, didn't I?"

Laura began to turn away without the answer, but Rose

pointed to the *Canada* painted on the back of the wagon, which had just come into view.

Smiling, Laura said, "Why, that wagon parked by the trees over there is from Canada."

Manly looked at the wagon and then at Laura. "Canada? How can you tell?"

Winking at Rose, Laura laughed, "Manly, if you'd look before you speak, you'd see the word *Canada* painted on the side."

Rose giggled at her father's discomfort. Manly, ten years older than Laura, was not as smart as his wife, but their likes and dislikes blended nicely on so many things that they were a well-matched pair in every other way.

What had attracted Laura to Manly was simple: He was just like her pa. Without a doubt, he had Pa's heart and soul. Pa and Manly both loved to sing and would always press ahead, no matter what the odds. They might not *plan* ahead, but they'd always press ahead when they were backed to the wall.

CHAPTER 2

"WHY WON'T YOU MARRY A FARMER?"

Laura was a pioneer girl. She'd never planned to be a farmer's wife. She'd been born in a log cabin and reared in wagons. She had memories filled with her pa's fiddle songs and the war whoops of painted Indians.

Laura had been raised on the road by a father just one dream away from the good life and one step in front of the hard times that had followed them. She had spent her life roaming all over the prairie, living in small houses.

Laura's first memory was of a cabin in the woods, which they soon left for other cabins and sod houses on the plains. Her favorite home of all had been the one on the prairie, which Pa had mistakenly built in Indian Territory.

As the wagon creaked forward, Laura looked over at Manly and closed her eyes, thinking back to the years he'd spent courting her. Manly had wanted to marry her the first time he'd seen her at the Congregational Church revival back in De Smet, South Dakota.

De Smet was a small, small town without much to do. Everyone had gone to the revival because everyone else was going. Laura had reluctantly gone along at the urging of her family. She didn't like prayer meetings much. When she prayed, she prayed in private, not in front of the whole town.

A young farmer named Manly Wilder caught Laura Ingalls's eye, but she was already interested in another boy, one who wasn't a farmer and talked of living in the city.

But Laura Ingalls was the only girl Manly wanted, so he persistently pursued her for years. Sometimes he had to drive his sleigh through miles of snowdrifts at forty below zero to come see Laura.

Manly took Laura on a lot of buggy rides because he needed a place to ask her to marry him—over and over and over again. She turned him down every time.

Manly was not one to accept no for an answer, but Laura was strong willed and outspoken, so different from all the polite, quiet girls he could have married.

Laura's ways, views, and brains scared off many of the other young men, which was all right with Manly. He could wait her out. She just kept eliminating the competition for him.

Then came the day of the buggy ride in the countryside near De Smet, South Dakota, when the buggy bumped and Laura fell against Manly's shoulder. Laura believed he bumped the buggy on purpose because he immediately tried to kiss her cheek. Laura just brushed him away.

Frustrated, Manly snapped the buggy whip above the horses. "Laura, why won't you marry a farmer?"

Straightening herself out and smoothing the lap robe to keep the dust off her pretty dress, Laura looked sternly into

Manly's eyes. "I don't want to marry a farmer because a farm is too hard a place for a woman. There are just too many chores to do. There's the cooking, the cleaning, feeding all the hired help, and no telling who you'd bring around."

"Oh, Laura," Manly said, disappointed.

" 'Oh, Laura,' yourself," she snapped. "I'm not going to end up saying my work prayer every day."

Manly shook his head. "What's wrong with prayin'?"

Laura got that certain stubborn look in her eye that Manly knew was a sign she was getting annoyed. "If this is all a woman has to pray for, God help us:

> Wash on Monday,
> Iron on Tuesday,
> Mend on Wednesday,
> Churn on Thursday,
> Clean on Friday,
> Bake on Saturday,
> Rest on Sunday."

Manly began to laugh because Laura was getting upset and looking all the more silly for it. "Sounds good to me," he said in a tone of voice he knew would annoy her more.

She looked at him and set her jaw. "The only poem for men should be:

> Yap on Monday,
> Mosey around on Tuesday,
> Poke around on Wednesday,
> Sneak a nap on Thursday,
> Smoke a pipe on Friday,

Go to town on Saturday,
Sleep on Sunday."

Turning away from Manly, she looked out over the countryside. "No, I'm not going to end up like my ma."

"And how's that?" Manly asked, with a "Well, look at you" expression.

Laura wasn't going for any of it. She snapped her fingers on the first word. "Broke. A farmer just never has any money. He can't make any because the merchants tell him what they'll pay for what he's got to sell."

She sat up and continued with determination. "Then they overcharge the farmer for what he needs to buy. Of course, he's planning to grow what they want to sell, but oh yes, those merchants are always gracious enough to give him credit at high interest rates." She paused to catch her breath. *"It's just not fair!"*

Laura was so lost in her thoughts that when the wagon bumped again, she fell against Manly's shoulder and startled him. At that moment he turned toward her and almost bumped into a wagon filled with happy Swedes that was in front of him.

Manly smiled and reached his arm around her. "Laura, you falling against my shoulder reminds me of that buggy ride where I finally agreed to marry you."

Laura looked at him with a flabbergasted look in her eyes. "Manly Wilder, it was *I* who finally agreed to marry *you!*"

Manly laughed and poked her in the ribs. Rose giggled from behind them, quite used to her father's games. Manly teased, "Aren't you glad you married me, Honeybee?"

When Laura didn't anaswer, Manly poked her again. "I said, aren't you glad you married me? Don't you remember that buggy ride where you agreed to say 'I do'?"

Laura crossed her arms. "Manly, take your mind off that buggy ride where my mind must have been possessed and I agreed to marry a farmer."

She looked over at Manly, who was grinning from ear to ear. He blew her an air kiss with his lips, which broke down all her defenses. The pioneer and the farmer were still together, on the road again, looking for a better life.

CHAPTER 3

THE MEMORIES LEFT BEHIND

$\mathcal{C}$ows trailing behind other wagons kept up a constant farm chorus around them. Resting her head on Manly's shoulder, Laura thought about life's broken promises and dead-end roads.

Laura could remember leaving her family's prairie home as if it were yesterday. She hadn't known where they were going, only that Pa had sold the cow and the calf and was leaving their wonderful house behind. He had mistakenly built their home in Indian Territory, a three-mile mistake that cost the Ingalls and the other families forced to move a million miles of broken dreams. Indians wanted the white men out, and the U.S. government was sending troops to evict the settlers as part of the treaty agreed to by Congress. There was no choice, Pa said. They had to go.

So they had packed up to leave. Laura and Mary had sat on the bed in the back, baby Carrie resting between them. Everyone was washed and in fresh clothes for the trip to who-knew-where.

When they were almost ready to leave, little Laura, overcome with emotion, had pleaded with Pa to let her look at the house just one more time.

Pa opened the back of the wagon cover, and Laura had stared at the house. It seemed to call Laura to stay. "Don't leave! This is your home! Why are you leaving?" All the fun and adventures of living there had flashed before her eyes, only to be dashed by the creaking of the wagon as Pa loaded the last trunk into the back.

Laura watched Pa open their home's door for one last look —at the flooring he had cut by hand, the furniture he'd made, the roof he had put on, which almost killed Ma when the beam he was placing fell on top of her.

Just one last look at the bedstead, the fireplace, and the expensive glass windows. Everything they had saved for was being left behind again. Ma was crying, trying to hide her tears.

Laura could hear Pa's lilting voice as they drove away, and he tried to get everyone to sing along to raise their spirits.

> Row away, row o'er the waters so blue,
> Like a feather we sail in our gum-tree canoe.
> Row the boat lightly, love, over the sea;
> Daily and nightly I'll wander with thee.

Laura had sung along, not putting her heart into it. She sang because it made Pa happy to hear her sing. She loved Pa. She didn't understand him, but she loved him with her heart and soul, nonetheless.

Before she and Manly married, Laura just wanted to escape the poverty that had always followed her family. Old Mr.

Poverty always seemed to catch up to them and pick their pockets clean. Her pa's best intentions had never been enough to pay the bills.

Manly had talked of riches, fine clothes, cash crops, and big houses—all hers if she would marry him. Though she hadn't wanted to be a farmer's wife, she had wanted security more than anything else.

Laura could remember Manly holding her hands that day when he stopped the buggy and looked into her eyes. "Laura, if you'll try being a farmer's wife for three years, and I haven't made a success in farming by that time, why, I'll quit and do anything you want me to do."

After their small, simple wedding, the local newspaper had written: "United in the journey of life. May their voyage be pleasant, their joys be many, and their sorrows few."

But only sorrows had visited Laura and Manly.

Their first year had led to the second and third, and soon the events that plagued them overwhelmed Laura. Crops failed. Their son died. The house burned down.

Mortgage debt forced them to move from house to cabin to shanty, until they were homeless and had to move in with relatives and take care of the cleaning and laundry in other people's houses. America became for them the land of the free and the home of people unable to pay their mortgages.

Crop failure, death, and disease: They had suffered it all. When Laura came down with a bad case of diphtheria, she followed doctor's orders and got better. Manly was also sick, but he stubbornly disregarded the doctor's orders and went out to work on the farm, saying there was "man's work to be done."

Well, the man overexerted himself, suffered a stroke, and

was left partially paralyzed and with a permanent limp. Bouts of weakness left Manly not quite able to do all the farm work, so Laura had to help chop wood, cut grass for hay, and take care of the livestock.

The girl who didn't want to marry a farmer had become a farmer herself. Laura knew God worked in mysterious ways, but this ironic turn of events was almost too much. She married a farmer and became a farmer herself.

Laura shook her head. "Laura Ingalls Wilder, pioneer farm woman," didn't sound very good to her ears.

The stench of dirty lambs, cooking food till her clothes stank of lard, and washing dirty dishes had never pleased her. As a matter of fact, Laura hated it all. It made her sick. But she'd hug and kiss one of those dirty lambs now to have back the house that burned down.

She hated the debts worst of all, the groveling for credit and loans. But she would gladly have endured a lifetime of it if she could just have her baby boy alive again.

The three-week-old baby was buried in the desolate fields of South Dakota, and now Laura was in a covered wagon again, headed into another state in an attempt to rebuild their lives. Someone had once told her that "The wheel goes round and round, and the fly on top will be the fly on the bottom after a while."

Well, Laura didn't give a hoot about being the top fly. She just wanted to climb up halfway, to get her fair share of life. Her wheel seemed stuck because she was a farmer's wife and farmers were always at the bottom, at the mercy of the system. Reaching under the wagon's seat, she picked up the old family Bible and began reading, "The Lord is my shepherd; I shall not want . . ."

CHAPTER 4

THE LETTER HOME

Shrugging off her melancholy mood, Laura took up her nickel notepad and began a letter to her friends and family back home. Manly always told her that "Everything will be all right, for it all evens up in time." In a strange way she sincerely believed he was right.

> *I thought our family and friends in De Smet, South Dakota, might like to hear how we are progressing on our long journey. We have had a pleasant trip so far, no bad weather to delay us, having had only a few light showers.*

Manly hit another bump, and Laura looked up. A double-teamed wagon was approaching. Manly gave them a warm "How do" and was answered in a mixture of French and English with a friendly wave in return.

A young boy with a knit cap peeked out from under the canvas of the wagon. From behind her parents' backs, Rose made a face at the boy and giggled at his reaction. Laura tapped Rose's shoulder, shaking her head in mild disapproval.

Then Laura continued her letter home.

> *The country is full of immigrants traveling in every direction. Our horses, though weary, are in good condition, and our wagon is whole, having had no accidents . . .*

Laura stopped, reread what she had just written, looked at Manly holding the reins, and added the word *yet*.

> *. . . having had no accidents yet. We have been on the road for forty-five days. After losing the child and Manly's stroke and bout with diphtheria, followed by losing the farm when the crops failed, having the house burn down, and having to work as a seamstress to pay the debts, perhaps this wagon ride is just what this pioneer girl needed.*
>
> *All we have left is a one-hundred-dollar bill to start again. I've got it tucked safely away in the wagon.*

Laura looked at Rose and Manly. She looked at the beautiful Missouri countryside, at the clouds and the birds overhead. She looked and saw life itself and felt ashamed at what she had written.

> *But yet, that's not really true. We have more than just a piece of paper. We've got Rose and our marriage and our faith. I remember, Ma, when you told me to*

always remember Psalm 121 when you travel. I still know it by heart.
   I love you all.

   Love Laura.
   Somewhere East of Springfield, Missouri.

As Manly tried to give another wagon room to pass, he edged too close to the side of the road, scraping against a small fieldstone wall. Laura looked up and said a silent prayer of thanks as the wheel cleared the rest of the wall.

As Manly moved the team back onto the center of the road, Rose pulled a plum from the sack under the seat and took a dripping, slurping bite. Manly turned, and Rose handed him a plum. Juice was soon dripping down his chin, too.

Laura reacted out of second nature, reaching over with her handkerchief and catching the drip off his chin before it hit his store-bought shirt.

As the wagon crested another hill, Manly halted the horses by a sign:

MANSFIELD, MISSOURI
LAND OF THE BIG RED APPLE

Manly took off his hat and wiped his brow. "Laura, this is sure beautiful country."

Below them, nestled among the Ozark hills, was a pretty rural village. Rose tugged at her mother's dress, pointing to the village. Laura looked up from her reading.

Manly put his arm around her. "Stop your writing,

woman, and just look at what God's created here in the Ozarks."

Laura looked around and was struck by it all. "Why, it's beautiful here, Manly."

Before he could answer, Laura looked down at her nickel notepad and began furiously writing.

Manly shook his head. "Now what have you written? Read it to me."

Laura held the nickel notepad up. "It says, *'This is where we stop.'* "

"This is where we stop? Here?" Manly asked.

"Yes, right here," she answered, nodding her head as she looked over the countryside.

Manly looked at her eyes closely. "Are you sure, Laura?"

Laura hugged Rose and reached over and kissed Manly on the cheek. "I'm sure! We're at the end of our journey!"

Manly started the team toward the town of Mansfield, Missouri—toward a new and hopefully better life.

As the buildings and people came clearly into view, Rose hugged her mother. "We're here, Momma. We're here at last. This is the magic place that you and Pa have been looking for."

Laura looked at her daughter and hugged her again. "Yes, Rose, we're home. I think we've finally found our home."

Manly began singing the song he always sang when he was filled with incurable optimism:

> You talk of the mines of Australia,
> They've wealth in red gold, without doubt;
> But, ah! there is gold in the farm, boys—
> If only you'll shovel it out.

Laura smiled and looked at her husband, thinking it could just as easily be Pa singing. She hoped that she had finally come to the end of her pioneer girl's journey, that Mansfield, Missouri, was the place she'd always been heading toward over the prairies of her life: home.

CHAPTER 5

WELCOME TO MANSFIELD

At the end of the nineteenth century, America was still a rural nation. The majority of people worked on farms. Forty-five million Americans, 60 percent of the population, lived in towns with fewer than twenty-five people.

They lived in towns like Mansfield, enduring the life-and-death grip of the seasons on farm life, living with Mother Nature's rhythms that affect the timing of planting and harvesting.

Mansfield, Missouri, was a progressive town. The people were hardy and the merchants normally fair. Those merchants that weren't fair didn't stay in business long. It was just that simple.

Though traveling immigrants had horrible tales to tell about the crooked merchants they'd run into in places like New York, it wasn't that way in Mansfield.

No one here would "weight the scales" with a small piece of lead to charge you more for your meat. The flour in the general store wasn't "stretched" with plaster. It just wasn't done. The cornmeal wasn't "flavored" with sawdust, and the black pepper didn't have any gypsum in it to "stabilize it." This was Mansfield, Missouri, not some big city.

A mixture of Germans, English, and French had settled this part of the Ozarks. There were Catholics, Methodists, Baptists, a few Mennonites, and some Mormons, who kept mostly to themselves.

As their wagon rolled into town, Laura stared at the store windows and commercial life around them. She'd lived her whole life away from neighbors in Pa's various houses and hadn't even seen her first town until she was nearly five years old!

A young boy ran beside the wagon, skipping along. "Where're you from, Mister?"

Manly responded in a nonchalant way, "West."

The boy looked perplexed. "West? West of where?"

Manly smiled. "Oh, west of here and north of there, a little east of this and a bit south of that."

The boy stopped and scratched his head.

Laura wagged her finger playfully in front of Manly's face. "Tell the boy where we're from."

Manly laughed. "We're the new Okies from South Dakota."

Manly brought the wagon to a halt in front of the general store. After tying the team, he lifted Rose from the back and helped Laura step down.

"I'm going over to the land office to inquire about any good farms for sale around here."

Laura squeezed his hand. "Manly, don't sign a mortgage until we discuss it. We've only got one hundred dollars left—just one hundred dollars to start again and survive on."

"I know, Laura. I know. This time I know what I'm doing."

They had not forgotten how he'd mortgaged them into disaster in the Dakotas against hopes of good crops to come. The only crop they had grown was a bumper crop of bad luck and disaster.

As Manly walked off to the land office, Laura and Rose looked at the display in the window of the Bedal General Store. The poster in the window proudly proclaimed:

THE PLACE TO BUY
GROCERIES, PROVISIONS,

BOOTS
AND
SHOES

CROCKERY, QUEENSWARE,
CANDY, CIGARS, DRESS CLOTH

And everything else usually kept in a
First-Class Country Store,
AT THE
Very Lowest Prices
FOR CASH OR COUNTRY PRODUCE IS,
at the old and well-known
BEDAL GENERAL STORE
Mansfield, Missouri

Stores like Bedal's were the link between the consumer and supplier. There were cans of Golden Cream Corn for eight cents displayed next to one-hundred-pound sacks of white sugar for five dollars. A pretty beaded purse for sixty cents caught Laura's eye, along with rolls of gingham and Madras cloth which would make pretty dresses for Rose, at ten cents a yard.

Rose stared at the dolls, small toys, and candy . . . bins and bins of candy of all colors—suckers, gumballs, stick candy, and sucking candy. Rose had never seen so much candy in her life.

Lafayette Bedal was the store's proprietor. A warm and hardy French-Canadian who had left Quebec, Canada, in search of adventure, he had settled down as a merchant in Mansfield.

He opened the front door and welcomed them inside with his warm French accent: "Please, ladies, please come in. I am Lafayette Bedal, owner and operator of this humble store."

Rose giggled at this display of chivalry, and Laura nodded her head. "Thank you, Mr. . . ."

"Bedal, Lafayette Bedal. I am a French-American by way of Canada."

Once inside, Laura was struck with that same feeling she always got entering a general store. Pa Ingalls had always settled within a day's ride of a country store. It had been their lifeline, supplying the basics for survival and the few luxuries that held special places in her memory.

As Laura looked around the store, she was lost in it all, as if the world had opened a store in front of her. In Mr. Bedal's general store there were coffee beans from South America and teas from China.

There was even some tea from India, nutmeg from Malay,

canned vegetable goods from Chicago, and seafood from New England. Shelves of patent medicines lined the side wall: Burdock Bitters, Sands Sarsaparilla, Wart Remover, Castor Oil, St. Jacob's Oil, Hair Balsam, Cough Syrup, and Wine of Cardui.

Rose just stared and stared at the penny candies. Her eyes were as big as the chocolate-covered drops. There were peppermint sticks, ribbon candies, horehound drops, chocolate babies, Wrigley's gum, and a candy that Laura had never seen before. It was called a Tootsie Roll.

Laura knew how Rose felt because Pa always bought her a piece of store-bought candy for Christmas. To the rich folks that might not sound like much, but to a pioneer girl miles and miles from nowhere, it was like the riches of the world.

Laura walked over and put her hand on Rose's shoulder. Tears rimmed Laura's eyes, and her heart hurt with each word. "Rose, dear, we can't afford that candy now. Every cent we have left has to go toward getting us a place to live."

Perhaps remembering the hard times of his own youth, Mr. Bedal opened the glass candy case and took out a long piece of red licorice. Without making a display of his friendly gesture, he came back around the counter and handed it to Rose. "This is for you, little angel."

Rose thanked him before she realized she hadn't asked her mother if it was all right to accept it. Laura, never one for unneeded charity, politely took the candy from Rose and handed it back. "I'm sorry, Mr. Bedal, but I can't be buying candy when we don't have a home."

"Well, lady, this isn't charity. This is common hospitality, just a . . ."

Never at a loss for words and always one with a twinkle in his eye for the ladies, Lafayette Bedal laughed and began speaking quickly in French. Laura and Rose didn't understand, so he stopped in midsentence.

"Sorry, sometimes I forget that Americans only speak one language." Seeing Rose stare at the candy in his hand, he handed it back to her. Patting Rose on the head he said, "Mrs. . . ."

"Wilder. Mrs. Laura Ingalls Wilder. And this is my daughter Rose."

"Ah, yes, Mrs. Wilder. As I was saying, your little girl looks just like an angel from heaven, so consider this candy a small gift, a sort of French-Canadian welcome to Mansfield, Missouri."

Rose's mouth was watering to take a bite—or even just a small lick. At that moment, just a nibble off the end was the most important thing in the world to Rose.

Laura began to object again but caught her tongue. This man was doing what she would be doing in his place. "Thank you, Mr. Bedal. We'll pay you back in some way."

Lafayette laughed. "Mrs. Wilder, it's only a penny. I can afford to be nice. I own the store."

Rose took a bite and Laura smiled. "Still, a penny saved is a penny earned. We'll pay you back in some way someday. I promise. That's the way I was raised."

Patting Rose on the head, Lafayette looked at Laura and smiled. "You must have Scottish blood, Mrs. Wilder."

"That I do, Mr. Bedal. That I do."

Lafayette Bedal was still laughing good-naturedly as they

left the store to find Manly. Taking her diary pad from the wagon, Laura quickly wrote:

I will one day repay Mr. Bedal for this small act of kindness. His wonderful welcome to Mansfield, Missouri, has touched me deeply.

CHAPTER 6

THE PROMISED LAND

Manly danced up behind Laura and spun her around. "It's all going to work out, girl!" He hugged her tight and kissed her before he set her down.

Laura, never one for public displays of affection, was clearly embarrassed. "Manly, Manly, are you having another bout of fever?"

Manly noticed Rose's piece of candy and began to ask a question, but stopped. Shrugging his shoulders in a "what will be will be" gesture, he danced a jig next to the wagon. People on the sidewalk snickered. Even the horses looked back at him.

Manly was his own person and couldn't have cared less that he was making a scene. "Laura, there's a place 'bout a mile outside of town that's for sale. Owner wants to sell something fierce. The man says . . ."

Laura stared at him. "Who says?"

"The man," Manly answered, dancing on one leg and reaching out for Laura to dance with him.

Laura was clearly not in the dancing mood. "What kind of man? A fireman? A preacherman? A policeman? A . . ."

"No, the man who's selling the land." Manly laughed, dancing away from her.

Laura grabbed his arm and stopped him. "Oh, you mean the *sales*man," she said, emphasizing the first half of the word.

"Yes," he said sheepishly, finally noticing the people who were snickering from the sidewalk.

Laura shook her head. "Okay, I just wanted to get it straight who was describing this great land deal."

Manly was not to be deterred. "Come on, Laura, this sounds like our dream place. It has hills, fruit trees, streams, crop land, a small house, and . . ."

"How much?" she asked quietly.

Manly tried to tease her. "How much what? Land? Why it's got about forty acres."

Laura was not in a playful mood. "No, Manly. How much does it cost?"

"Why, just three hundred dollars." He beamed a sunshine smile.

Laura's mouth dropped. "Three hundred dollars! Manly, have you lost your mind? We only have one hundred!"

Manly looked down and kicked his shoe against his pants leg. "Man said he'd take a mortgage."

Laura's voice was sharp. "Mortgage must be your middle name. 'Manly Mortgage Wilder.' Or maybe your name should be 'Mortgage Manly' or 'Mortgage Wildly'."

Hurt showed in Manly's eyes and he got defensive. "Everyone takes a mortgage. We ain't all Vanderbilts or Morgans in this country."

"And we never will be, the way you handle money!" quipped Laura. "We've only got one hundred dollars to feed and clothe the family, and you want to go and spend it all on a sight-unseen farm."

He shook his head. "You're wrong, Laura! You're just plumb wrong."

"I am?" she asked, raising her eyebrows at the serious look on his face.

Manly smiled. "Course we're going to see it before we buy it. I'm doing all this for you, Laura. Don't you know that?"

As he stood there with hound-dog eyes, scuffing his shoes on his pants leg, Laura could see the little boy in her husband—full of life, full of enthusiasm, and full of hot air a lot of the time. But Manly meant well.

She softened her tone. "I'm just worried, that's all."

Manly inched up and kissed her cheek. "I know, Honeybee, but will you just take a look? If you don't like it, we won't buy it."

Laura closed her eyes and grinned. "Take me to see this place. I'll try to keep an open mind."

Manly broke out in a yell and danced a jig again. "I know you're going to love it. I just know it!"

They got back in the wagon and headed toward another of Manly's adventures.

He brought the wagon to a halt on a not-very-promising piece of ground. The land was covered with sassafras, sharp thickets, steep slopes, ledges, and heavy, heavy woods.

He checked his directions again. "Yup, this is the place."

Rose hopped out, and Jack the dog went running and barking through the brush. At the top of the tree-covered ridge stood a primitive cabin, halfway between standing up and falling down.

Below them was a deep, rocky ravine. A clear spring-fed

creek meandered around the base of the hill. An orchard of apple trees, left to rot, stood on the hillside.

"Well, Laura, what do you think?" Manly asked hopefully.

"Give me a moment, please," she said quietly, folding her hands.

Laura looked around, not saying anything. She heard the birds, felt the breeze, and saw the stream. All the wonders of creation were in front of her, but she could also see the little log shack on the hill. It was smaller than the first house Manly had moved her into when they first got married.

Manly cleared his throat. "Laura? What do you think?"

Laura put her face in her hands and tried to regain her composure. "I don't know, Manly. I'm so overwhelmed."

Mistaking her letdown for elation, Manly just went right along with himself. "I knew you'd like it, Laura. Man said it's good land here. It might not have smooth, wide fields of wheat, but we got ourselves some apple trees. Why, we can clear some land, plant some grass, raise ourselves some cattle, and . . ."

Laura took her hands from her face. Manly now realized that these were not tears of joy. "And . . . you can have hens and a garden and . . ."

Laura interrupted him. "And a shack."

Manly laughed. "Come on, Laura, you ain't even seen it yet."

"I don't have to see it. A shack is a shack, Manly. That place looks like a compost dump."

"Pshaw, woman, you ain't even seen it yet!"

Hopping down from the wagon without Manly's help, Laura brushed back her hair. "Okay, Manly, let's see the house we traveled a thousand miles to find."

Rose skipped ahead of them as they walked up the ridge. Manly had a worried look on his face as he limped along. He felt like the pirate being forced to "walk the plank" in a story Rose had read to him.

The house *was* a sight to see. Actually, it was a sight that Laura had hoped she would never see again.

At the door she was overcome with emotions. She remembered another door, Pa's door. How carefully Pa had worked, building the door for their prairie house. He had measured, cut, and trimmed the wood to a perfect fit. The hinges hung tight. The door was secure, to keep the warmth in and the Indians out.

Laura could remember the quality of Pa's door as she pulled on the latch, but she was brought back to reality when the shanty door came off its hinge.

"Er, I can fix that easy, Laura. Don't you worry," Manly stammered.

Laura stepped inside the one-room cabin. Dust and dirt were everywhere. There were no windows. It would have been very stuffy except for the hole in the roof. A squirrel looked down on them.

Rose looked up at the hole in the roof. "Is it going to leak in here, Momma?"

Laura shook her head. "No, Rose, it's not going to leak in here. Leak? No, when it rains, it's sure going to rain in here. But leak? No, it will all leak outside!"

Laura broke into one of those silly laughs that always come at the wrong time. Yes, it was going to leak in this cabin! It was going to rain cats and dogs until Manly could figure a way to fix it.

The cabin was built from logs and held together by

wooden pins, gravity, and luck. A good workman could build a snug home. Pa could. This one was more like a sieve and was about as tight as the end of a loose woodpile. A broken-down "prairie rascal" primitive bed was in the corner, along with a cracked rough-hewn table and two chairs without legs.

After inspecting the cabin, Laura walked the property. If she could just make herself forget about the condition of the cabin, she had to admit that the land *did* have promise. There were fruit trees and streams and a heavenly breeze, which seemed to cool every inch of the property.

Laura stopped to look at her reflection in the creek. She was no teenage bride anymore. She was twenty-seven going on fifty and feeling very tired. There was no easy way around what faced them if they bought the place. If they were to live here, the work had to be done one step at a time.

Laura took Manly's hand and slowly walked up to the top of the ridge. She slowed her naturally fast step to accommodate his limp. At the top of the rock-strewn ridge, Laura surveyed it all. It was pretty here. Yes indeed, it was certainly pretty country.

The land tugged at her heart. There was something very special about the place.

Rose hugged her mother's leg. "Momma? Momma, are we going to live here? Are we, Momma?"

Manly hesitantly repeated the question. "Are we, Momma?"

Purposely putting a frown on her face, Laura shook her head as if answering no. Manly's face dropped. Tears welled up in Rose's eyes.

With a poke in Manly's ribs, Laura broke into a big grin. "Yes, this is our new home."

Rose shrieked with joy, Jack barked, and Manly danced another jig.

"What are we going to call it, Momma?" Rose asked. "What are we going to call our new home?"

Laura looked around. The apple trees caught her eye. They would live—wanted to live—if someone took care of them. She stepped up onto the biggest boulder at the highest point and lifted her arms to the breeze.

"We're going to call it . . . Apple Hill Farm."

CHAPTER 7

THE DOWN PAYMENT

Manly was so excited that he quickly unpacked most of the wagon and told Laura he was going to go to town and buy the place. All he needed was the hundred-dollar bill and they'd have a new home with fruit trees and forty acres.

"Just get out the money, Laura. Time's a-wasting. I don't want anyone else to snap this place up from under our feet."

Laura lifted down another crate of household items. All Manly needed was the hundred-dollar bill. All he needed was all the money they had left in the world.

"Manly, there's nobody going to be rushing to buy this place. Who'd want it, except for some silly fools from the Dakotas who don't know any better?"

Manly laughed. "You know I love you, Laura! I'll make you happy here."

Laura sighed and lifted down another crate. "Just feed and take care of us, Manly. That's all I ask."

Manly was elated. "I'll plant the garden, and we'll live like kings!"

Laura rolled her eyes at his promise and thought, *Men! What can you do about them?*

After unpacking the last crate and walking Laura and Rose up to the shanty, Manly wiped his brow. He paced nervously, scuffing his feet in the dirt. "Okay, Laura, give me the money, and I'm off to town to lay claim to our new home."

Laura opened a sack, looking in absent-mindedly. "It won't be ours until we pay off the mortgage. Two hundred dollars for a mortgage is a lot of money."

Manly scoffed impatiently. "We've had higher."

Laura replied sadly, "And we've fallen that much further. Remember, we lost one farm to an unpaid mortgage."

"Come on, Laura, that's all behind us now. You know I know better now, don't you?" he asked with outstretched hands.

Laura shook her head in doubt. Old dogs don't learn new tricks easily, and old fools are worse when it comes to handling money. But Manly wasn't an "old" fool, so maybe there was still hope for him.

She took out the sewing kit where she'd carefully hidden the hundred-dollar bill. Picking through the spools of thread, under the needle sheet, and inside the measuring cloth, she searched carefully.

"It's in here somewhere," Laura whispered to herself. "Probably inside the piece of folded gingham. No, not there. Maybe it's inside the secret hole in the lining. No. Well, maybe it . . ."

It wasn't there! Their life savings were gone! Laura was frantic.

Manly grabbed her hand. "What's wrong, Laura?"

Tears spilled from her eyes. "Manly, I can't find it."

Manly heard what she said but didn't want to accept it. "Can't find what?"

Laura poured out the contents of the sewing box. "The money! I can't find our money."

No matter how hard they searched, it was not to be found. For the next three days they literally tore the wagon apart. They wracked their brains to recall how they could have lost or misplaced it. How could it have been stolen? How could they have lost it? Laura felt the responsibility of their family's future on her shoulders because she had hidden the money herself.

On the evening of the third day, Laura sat on her rocker, which was their only piece of furniture. As she rocked, she repeated over and over the first line of the psalm she always said when facing a crisis: "God is our refuge and strength, a very present help in trouble. . . ."

Manly looked up. "Laura, it will be all right. We'll get by. I'll take a job in town and learn to sell dry goods or something."

Laura felt so guilty. She had been so hard on Manly, blaming him for everything, but she never saw her own faults. Here was a man willing to give up farming for her, and all she could do was brood, sulk, and cry. "Manly, I'm sorry. I just don't know what happened to the money. I've searched and I've prayed, but I can't find it."

As she lifted up the big family Bible from the wagon box next to her, Manly smiled and said, "We'll get by. We always have. I'll go earn the money and buy you another house somewhere—why, maybe even a house in town. That's right! I'll be a butcher, Rose will be a baker, and you can be a candlestick maker. How'd you like that, girl?"

Laura smiled at Manly's refusal to be defeated by anything. The big family Bible was heavy on her lap. Opening the pages, looking sadly for words of hope, she noticed that one page in Psalms was folded inward on itself. Hidden inside the fold was their hundred-dollar bill!

She held it up to show Manly, who let out a soft whistle of relief before breaking out in another boyish jig of joy. Clutching the hundred-dollar bill in her hand as the fire cast its light on the pages of the family Bible, Laura bowed her head. "Thank you, Lord," she said softly. They would never know how the bill came to be in the Bible instead of in the sewing kit.

CHAPTER 8

FROM LAURA'S DIARY

So we bought Apple Hill Farm and went to work. We used our one hundred dollars as the down payment and took a mortgage of two hundred dollars. Because of what had happened in De Smet, I was constantly worried about money. We had very, very little except our bare hands with which to pay it off, and Manly, with his broken health, and I managed to do the work rebuilding the orchards.

It was a while before we could get any hens, and Manly was dreaming about having a chicken pie. I remembered Ma surprising Pa one time with blackbird pie and Pa saying, "Ma, it takes you to think up a chicken pie a year before there's chickens to make it with."

So I had traded a neighbor some apples for a string of blackbirds he had shot and made a blackbird pie. It was hard cutting the birds in half without a meat cleaver, but I managed. I mixed in a wild onion and the only clove I had left, rigged up an oven of sorts, and made Manly a pie.

I even served it singing like Ma had . . .

> Sing a song of sixpence
> A pocket full of rye.
> Four and twenty blackbirds
> Baked in a pie . . .

Manly laughed and used the johnnycakes to wipe his plate clean. I still don't know why it's called johnnycake when it's not a cake at all. Just bread made from cornmeal and water paste, spread on a board, and baked in front of the open fire.

Anyway, we soon had ourselves a flock of hens, and the wood we cleared from the land bought all our groceries and clothing. The timber on the place also made rails to fence it and furnished the materials for a large log barn.

When Mr. Bedal visited I baked him an apple pie as a sort of "Welcome to Apple Hill Farm." I'll never forget how kind he was to Rose and me that first day we arrived. I put a penny in an envelope, and when he looked inside, he laughed!

When we bought the farm, there were four acres cleared and a small log house with a fireplace and no windows. It reminded me of so many of the other houses I'd lived in. There were practically no improvements, and there was not grass enough growing on the whole forty acres to keep a cow.

The four acres cleared had been set out to apple trees, and enough trees to set twenty acres more were in nursery rows near the house. The land on which to set them was not even cleared of the timber. It was hard work and sometimes short rations at first, but gradually the difficulties were overcome. It took a while

*to settle into our cabin, but with a little sweeping,
cleaning, and painting, it has come to have the feel of a
real home.*

*We've been introduced to some good neighbors
who've helped with some of the hard work. Down the
road live the Springers, a black family. Maurice
Springer has really been a blessing, and his wife, Eulla
Mae, has a lot of good country common sense.*

*Manly has been selling firewood in the town and has
brought back hens for me to raise. Jack chases the
squirrels and sometimes sits by the wagon as if
expecting us to hit the trail again. I hope that the trail
has ended here at Apple Hill Farm.*

*Neighbors helped us raise the barn, and we in turn
have helped them with their needs. "Fair is fair" is a
policy that makes good neighbors.*

*We were introduced at Rev. Youngun's church, but we
haven't been able to give much in the offering. Rev.
Youngun says not to worry, just to give what we can.
So I've given my time, my eggs, and Manly's chopped
wood as I've been able.*

*Every extra cent we've saved has gone to building up
this farm. And all we have left is a single dollar bill.*

CHAPTER 9

IT'S GOING TO BE ALL RIGHT

Laura worked hard to prepare the family meals. Food had always been an important part of Laura's life, as it was for all pioneer families. Most of her life had been spent hunting, growing, preserving, or eating food. Feeding the Ingalls family had always been a full-time job for Laura's parents. It was no different for her family now.

The kitchen in the cabin nestled in the hills of Missouri was part of the sitting room, bedroom, dining room, and Manly's workshop. There was only one room for everybody to do everything. It was pretty primitive compared to the kitchens shown in the new Sears catalog, but Laura made the best of it.

Laura liked to flip through the Sears-Roebuck pages and look at all the dresses and kitchen utensils while she sat in the outdoor privy. Manly must have flipped through it, too, because the tool section was always bent and folded every which way.

What upset Laura most was that Manly would rip out the pages from the ladies' section when he concluded his business in the outhouse. He never used the gun pages, never used the wagon pages—just the pages from the ladies' section. There must be some deep hidden meaning there, Laura felt.

Once she almost had a fit when she caught Manly walking off to the outhouse with the latest *Good Housekeeping* in his hand. Manly didn't read much and couldn't see why she was raising such a fuss. He had business to do and needed something to finish it with since the "Ol' helpful Mr. Sears' book" was about used up.

Laura began working on the fried salt pork dinner. Without any pigs of their own, they bought their pork from the butcher shop in town.

"Laura," Manly said, looking in through the front door, "when are we going to eat?"

Laura turned and smiled. "It's coming, Manly. We'll be eating soon."

By the time the plates were set, Manly was waiting to eat. Rose said the blessing, and before the last word was out of her mouth, he was pushing one of the corn dodgers through the pork drippings.

After dinner, Manly took his plate from the rough-cut table to the washing pot and stood in the doorway, staring at the woods. "When we get some crops planted, we'll be living like kings. Yes-sirree, we'll be living like the Rock-e-fellers."

Laura had heard her pa say the same thing right before disaster struck. As she tucked Rose in, she hoped that this time they would make it. The straw bed in the corner with the sheet in front was Rose's magic bedroom. Behind the curtain she played her games and read of places far, far away —just as Laura had done as a little girl. Laura hoped that Rose's dreams would come true.

By the flickering fireplace, Laura looked at their meager savings—a dollar bill, a dime, and a penny. The dime was for the church, the penny was for the poor box in town, and the dollar was all they had left to their name.

Laura knelt by the fire with a sigh of despair. Would they make it here, or would they fail once more and be forced to move on, leaving another home behind? Slowly she felt her worries lifted from her back. Her heart calmed, and she felt a peace she had not felt for years. "It's going to be all right," she whispered softly. "I *know* it's going to be all right."

CHAPTER 10

HOME IMPROVEMENTS

The Ozarks, 1904.

After a decade of hard work, Laura finally had her best house of all. The Ozark farmhouse was now bigger than all her other houses combined!

It had not been easy. Manly had used the timber on the land to make fence rails and posts. To earn money to build a new house on the property, he sold firewood in Mansfield for seventy-five cents a wagon load.

A year after they'd moved in, the first crops were planted. Little Rose helped plant the corn and picked blueberries on the hillsides, selling them in Mansfield for nine cents a gallon. Laura sold her apples, potatoes, and eggs, and with the money she bought a cow and pig. The cow meant fresh milk and butter.

During the second year, Manly built a nice one-room frame house at the top of the hill. They added more acres as they could afford it and eventually owned two hundred acres, eighty of them cleared.

Laura wrote in her diary:

*Apple Hill Farm has supplied everything necessary
for a good living and has given us good interest on all
the money invested every year. It is now worth $3,000
more than when we bought it.*

*We are not through making improvements on Apple
Hill Farm. But when I look around the farm now and
see the green, rolling meadows and pastures, our
thriving orchards, the fields of corn, wheat, and oats,
I know we were meant to be farmers.*

They were farmers, all right. With their orchard, hogs,
sheep, cattle, and goats, the Wilders were known throughout
Wright County as good farmers who produced quality food.
They produced big, tasty apples, which they shipped by the
train carload to St. Louis and Memphis.

One room became two, two became ten, and soon the
house really was bigger than all Laura's childhood houses
combined. Manly wanted everything she wanted—a Montgomery Ward cookstove and sink, a paneled parlor, special
wallpaper. Perhaps he wanted it to make up for the first
terrible four years and give Laura the lifetime of happiness
he felt she deserved.

If he couldn't buy it, he built it: cupboards, shelves, book-
cases, tables, chairs, a kitchen pass-through to the dining
room, and a study just for Laura and her books. Laura in-
sisted on using the three biggest boulders she'd found on the
property for the fireplace, and even though Manly couldn't
imagine how he'd get them there, with a little ingenuity and
elbow grease, the boulders were put in place. Apple Hill
Farm had become an Ozarks showplace, with the house that
Laura had dreamed about all her life.

Life was good on Apple Hill Farm, and by the summer of 1904, America was a land of peace and prosperity. Everyone in the country was singing "In the Good Old Summertime," the song made famous by George "Honey Boy" Evans.

Even Manly was humming it as he limped into Laura's writing room and hugged her, handing her a bag of chocolates. "Here's some sweets for my sweet."

Laura licked her lips, knowing how good the chocolates would taste and what they could do to her somewhat matronly thirty-seven-year-old figure. "I'd better not, Manly. I'm trying to lose weight."

Manly laughed. "Laura, all you got to do is wear one of them iron corsets, pull your waist in 'til it touches your backbone, then eat all the chocolates you want!"

Laura huffed. "I wouldn't wear one of those death traps if I was the fat lady in the circus." Putting the bag of candy down, she added, "I'll save these for Rose's next visit."

"Suit yourself," Manly shrugged, leaving the room.

Before he was through the door, Laura popped a candy in her mouth and chewed happily away.

It had been sad saying good-bye to Rose and seeing her only during the holidays. Though the schools in Mansfield were good, Laura wanted the best possible education for her daughter. It was hard sending her to live with relatives in New Orleans to attend the excellent high school down there, but Rose had blossomed into a real scholar.

Rose had also become a Gibson girl, which was all the rage in big cities like New Orleans. The Gibson girl was always tall and stately. You never saw her unless she was well-dressed. Rose said that in her room in New Orleans she had Gibson girl wallpaper, pillows, plates, and bowls.

Manly thought it was just another Yankee plot to get all the farm girls all riled up about leaving home. But Laura knew her daughter was going through the wonderful period in a young girl's life when everything seems so alive.

Later that evening Laura joined Manly on the front porch. Manly came and stood beside her. "Laura, our little farm has come a long way."

There was something bothering her, and this was the perfect opportunity to say it. "It's come a long way, Manly, but we still don't have running water."

"Running water? I keep telling you that the creek's downhill and we're uphill. And besides, carrying buckets of water is good exercise."

He patted her tummy just to poke fun at her refusal to eat his candy. She pushed his hand away and said, "I don't care. Those ladies who live in town have running water, but we don't. Aren't you getting tired of packing water to the house and barn every day?"

"Laura, you're always wantin' somethin' new. Look what I've already gotten you." He took her by the arm and pointed out all the Sears and Montgomery Ward inventions, contraptions, and combobulations that he'd bought for Laura to imitate the "good city life" she read about in her magazines.

Laura wouldn't budge. "Yes, Manly, I know we've got a new stove and fancy cook pans. And, yes, we have a gasoline engine that pumps water, turns the washing machine, and even runs my sewing machine. That's all fine and dandy, but—"

"But what, Laura?" Manly said, shaking his head.

Laura turned away, then whirled around. "I want running water in my sink."

A few weeks later, while Laura was seated in her study, Manly was downstairs, turning the new faucet on and off and admiring his handiwork.

They celebrated the running water and Rose's return from school with a roast pig dinner and mincemeat pie.

Manly carried the roasted pig to the table like a waiter in a fancy restaurant. Then he cut off the pig's head, knifed down the spine, and cut the pig in two halves. Manly wanted spareribs; Rose wanted shoulder meat; and Laura wanted ham.

After dinner Manly limped into her study. "Well, Laura," he said, feeling very proud of himself, "how's it feel to have running water like the city folks?"

Picking up her Sears catalog "wish book," she began absent-mindedly turning the pages, stopping here and there. "Really, Manly, I don't know how we ever managed without it."

While Manly looked out the window, Laura stopped on page 203 and began reading aloud to herself. "There are no telephones made at any price that will talk plainer or farther than our telephones. There are no telephones made at any price that will ring more bells on a line or that will ring over a greater distance than our telephones. Only $9.95." She put the catalog down. "Imagine that, Manly!"

Manly hadn't been listening. "What, Laura?"

Slapping the book, she nodded agreement with her thought. "That's what I want."

Turning to face her with an exasperated look on his face, Manly asked, "What now, Laura? I just worked my fingers to the bone getting you running water in the house. What else could a woman want?"

She smiled playfully. "Make a guess. It's got a bell and a cord."

Manly scratched his chin. "Hmm . . . bell and a cord . . . let's see. I got it!"

"What do you think it is?" she asked, trying to read his expression.

Manly said, with a straight face, "I don't know why you need another cow, but if you want one, I'll get you one with the biggest bell in the county."

Laura kept the game going and responded as if she were talking to a schoolboy. "A cow? My lands, Manly! Guess again. Sometimes I think farmers have peas for brains."

"Give me another clue," he requested with a determined look in his eye.

Laura almost burst out laughing, but restrained herself. "Okay, it helps women communicate with each other."

Manly saw a chance to jump back into control of the game and get a zinger in. "Well, let's see. You've already got a pretty—" (he coughed into his hand and said the word *"big"* so she couldn't hear it)—"mouth, so that can't be it. And you've already got a hen's gabbing club."

Stopping suddenly, he paled. He looked down at the Sears catalog. It was open to the phone ad that Laura had read.

He looked up and simply said, "No."

"Yes!" she shouted, clapping her hands.

"You don't really," Manly said in a dead-serious tone.

"I really do. I want a telephone like the ladies in *Good Housekeeping* have to call each other up on."

For a moment Manly was dumbstruck. Then he burst out, "A telephone! That dadgum Mr. Graham Bell. Why couldn't he have invented something useful, like an automatic cow caller or a working man's electric back scratcher?"

Laura walked over and scratched his back. "All I want is a telephone, Manly. Just a simple telephone that goes 'ring-ring' . . . and all you have to do is figure out how to get the phone line from town out to here."

Manly walked from the room shaking his head. "Oh, dear Lord, what will this woman want next?"

Laura whispered, "How about the right to vote?"

CHAPTER 11

PROTECT THE LAND

On Sunday mornings before church, Laura always made buttermilk pancake men with blueberry eyes, her favorite breakfast since she was a child.

With a flick of her wrist, Laura spooned the batter around, making first the legs, then the arms, and finally the head. She always made Manly a chubby pancake man that took up the whole griddle.

Sitting down to a plateful of pancake men covered with maple syrup and a hot sausage ball on the side, Manly said, "Laura, I hope when we're in heaven together that you'll make this for me every mornin'!"

Laura looked over from the hot stove. "That doesn't sound like heaven to me. Sounds more like a *man's* version of heaven."

"You know what I mean, Honeybee," he said, chewing on half a sausage ball.

"I know exactly what you mean, Manly Wilder. Men have created their own heaven on earth at women's expense. Don't be too sure that it's that way in heaven."

"I think God understands what men and women need," he said, stuffing the leg of a pancake man into his mouth.

Pouring the rest of the batter into the pan, Laura made a pancake devil with horns and a tail. Sliding it onto Manly's plate, she stepped back and smiled. "If you keep up that kind of talk, this is where you're going to go."

Manly peered at the pancake. "That looks like a pancake devil!"

"That's right," she laughed. "It'll be so hot down there that everything will cook by itself!"

Sunday church was a time to meet and greet their friends. Actual preparations began the night before with their Saturday-night bath. By the time they were ready to leave, Manly had his starched church shirt and tie on, and Laura and Rose were in their Sunday dresses.

They always took the best buggy to go to church in town. Along the way they waved to neighbors who answered in English mixed with their native tongues. They were all either on their way to worship or returning from church.

Laura fussed with her hair, trying to keep it in place. Manly just shook his head. "You know, if you'd wear a hat like the other ladies do, your hair wouldn't get so messed up."

Laura pushed a front lock of hair off to the side. "Don't like hats, Manly. I just don't like 'em."

"I think they look nice," he said with a gleam in his eye. "Even you'd look nice in a feathered hat."

Rose, home from school, giggled from the back, and Manly gave her a wink.

Laura would have none of the game. "Well, I'll get you one with fruits and birds' nests on it with a few pink ostrich feathers sticking out, and you wear it to town and see how you like it."

Rose laughed from the seat behind. "I think you'd look cute, Father. You might start a movement."

"Yeah, the men in the town might just move me out of town!" Manly snickered.

"Oh, Father, you would look so fashionable in a pink feathered hat," Rose chuckled.

"I've always said that if it chirped, women would wear it," Manly laughed.

Laura turned to look him in the eye. "That's unfair—you make it sound like women and birds are the same."

Manly had her now! He winked again at Rose. "That's why they say women have birdbrains!"

Laura had stepped into his trap and laughed good-naturedly. Though ladies' hats were all the rage, Laura didn't like them. Covered with lace, yards of ribbon, bouquets of flowers, or bunches of fruit—it didn't matter. She just didn't like them.

She also agreed with the Audubon Society that they were wasteful. At one auction selling bird feathers for ladies' hats, over twenty-four thousand egrets were laid out for sale. That made Laura sick.

Why, the Sears catalog had more than seventy-five pages devoted to hats. If you didn't want egret feathers, you could have the feathered remains of red-winged blackbirds, purple grackles, orioles, skylarks, pigeons, turtledoves, wrens, or thrushes.

Around the bend near town, Laura saw several ruined fields where the land had been abused. Good land wasted. It had been overplanted and was now left to ruin, with the wind carrying away its once fertile soil.

On the crest of the hill, Laura asked Manly to halt the buggy. "Look at that, Manly," she said, pointing to the woods to the left. The timber cutters had stripped them without thought to replanting. "Manly, it's a crime to treat good land like that!"

Manly "giddiyapped" the horses. "I know it, Laura. But it's their land to do with what they please."

Laura frowned and crossed her arms. "No, it's not!"

"I know it upsets you, Laura, but he who holds the deed owns the land."

"Isn't that right, Mother?" Rose asked.

Laura shook her head back and forth. "No, no, no! No one has the right to abuse land. It's like stealing from the future."

Farther down the road there was a sign in front of a field of stumps:

COUNTY DISEASE CONTROL PROGRAM
CONTRACT AWARDED TO:

LAND AND TIMBER COMPANY
WILLIAM BENTLEY, OWNER

Rose shook her head. "Mother, it doesn't make sense to cut down trees to save trees and then not replant trees."

"If there's disease on the trees, they got to cut 'em down, or else all the other trees will die," Manly answered.

"But shouldn't they replant?" Rose asked.

"Guess it depends on who owns the land," Manly said, wishing he'd taken a different route into town.

"Rose, some people think they own the future," Laura said as she looked at the barren field, "but they're wrong."

"Bentley's a powerful man in these parts," Manly said, snapping the reins to move the horses faster. He wanted to get Laura away from what was upsetting her.

William Bentley, the richest man around, controlled the county's timber industry. He was a big, tough man who could handle an axe as easily as an accountant's pen—handsome, arrogant, and ruthless. Even the people who didn't work for him stayed clear of him.

Bentley's wife, Sarah, was from New York City, which she always managed to bring up in any conversation. It was just her way of putting the people of Mansfield in their place. If the truth were known, most people in Mansfield wished she'd go back!

At the Methodist church, Manly carefully eased the buggy into an open spot. "See that buggy over there?" he said, pointing to a fancy one coming up the church drive. "That's Bentley and his snobby old wife, Sarah, and—" he paused, looking at the sissified boy in the back, "and their little snotty son, William Bentley, Jr."

Laura straightened up and stuck out her chin. "I'm going to walk over and say something to Mr. Bentley right now. I think it's about time someone stood up to him."

Manly moaned. "No, Laura, please no. Not on Sunday."

Manly was right. As they walked past the Bentleys' wagon, Laura couldn't help but look over. Sarah Bentley was lifting her silk lap robe off her fancy silk and silver-buttoned dress. She was wearing what appeared to be a fifty-dollar hat and a new pair of shoes. Looking at Laura, she stuck her nose in the air and snubbed her.

"Don't let her bother you none, Laura," Manly whispered. "She thinks she's all hotty-totty 'cause she's from New York."

Rose added her two-cents' worth. "Mother, she just thinks we're all hayseeds and half-wits around here—that everyone from west of New York is from the wrong side of the tracks."

Manly mumbled, "If she'd just go sit a spell on the tracks, some eastbound train would explain it all to her."

"Oh, Father," Rose said, shaking her head.

Manly made a face at his daughter. "Oh, Father, yourself! That woman is like all the rest of the snobby rich folks who act like they've birthed their own ancestors."

"Her attitude is her problem," huffed Laura. "I hope she doesn't try and join our ladies club. I've never blackballed anyone, but I just might start with her."

Rev. Youngun was greeting his parishioners as they entered. Standing behind the minister were his three children, squirming in their Sunday clothes: Larry, nine; Terry, six; and four-year-old Sherry. It had been a year since the fever took his wife, Norma, and it hadn't been easy being an underpaid preacher raising three kids alone.

Laura knew that children were considered assets for farmers, but wondered if that were true for Rev. Youngun. From the look on his face and the lines under his eyes, Laura suspected that the widower's life was not easy on him.

Larry, who wore his hat sideways, was the strong, quiet one. He didn't like to fight but protected his brother and sister from any trouble, though his real problem was with the local girls who liked him.

Terry was the red-haired devilish one, always instigating mischief. Small for his age but with a wise mouth, he depended on Larry to get him out of scrapes. Terry always had a dime novel about some outlandish cowboy story stuck in his back pocket. Laura knew he read it during the service, hiding it inside his Bible.

Terry had beautiful auburn hair, so a lot of the kids nicknamed him "Red." One day he took a can of white paint behind the barn and painted his auburn hair white. He thought it looked so good that he took off all but his under-breeches and painted his body white. His pa, Rev. Youngun, was fit to be tied and gave little Terry a bath in turpentine.

Sherry was the silly one. She'd sneak up to you and whisper, "Let me tell you a secret," and then she'd burp in your ear! Little Sherry would not be going to any more of her father's tent revivals. At the last one she had stood on her chair, screaming "Hallelujah" every time her father spoke about the power of sin.

On this particular day, the Rev. Youngun was oblivious to the antics going on behind him. Even if he'd seen them, he probably couldn't have stopped them, because as soon as he turned back around, they were at it again.

As Laura greeted the minister, he stepped aside and took her by the arm. "Laura, I need your help after the service."

Laura was puzzled. "What, Reverend Youngun? Whatever you need."

CHAPTER 12

LAURA SPEAKS HER MIND

Rev. Youngun told Laura, "We'd planned on having the traveling minister from the next county address the after-service gathering, but he's come down ill and can't speak. I want you to take his place, Laura."

Laura's throat constricted. "But I've never spoken to a group like that before."

Taking her arm and walking back to the church steps, the Rev. Youngun said, "You've spoken to the church ladies about so many issues that it's time you shared your thoughts with the rest of us."

Before entering the church, Laura stopped Rev. Youngun. "But what will I speak about?"

Rev. Youngun smiled. "Whatever comes to your mind, Laura. Whatever comes to mind."

Laura was not pleased. "I didn't plan anything. The thought is making me sick to my stomach."

"Just talk, Laura," Rev. Youngun chuckled. "That's all. Let it come from your heart. They all know you. They're your neighbors. Trust me—the good Lord will help you find the words in your heart."

A old woman pulled at his sleeve. "Be right with you." He whispered into Laura's ear, "Just remember what the Baptists say: The hardest part is waking up the audience after the person who introduces you has finished his remarks. I'll wake 'em up for you."

Laura sat through the service with a dozen wild, unnetted butterflies in her stomach. She hardly heard the sermon, and Manly had to remind her to bow her head at the right times. Laura didn't even notice the mouse hanging on the bell rope near the back of the church.

Larry Youngun saw it and poked Terry, who nudged Sherry.

"That mouse must be anxious to pray," whispered Larry.

"It's a church mouse," giggled Sherry.

After the service, the congregation gathered in the social room, expecting to hear the traveling minister. A pretty middle-aged widow named Carla Pobst from Cape Girardeau, Missouri—which was on the other side of the state—was introduced as a new member of the community. Rumor had it that the widow was left some money. With her dark hair and flashing eyes, she certainly caught the attention of the single men in the room.

Laura was sure that Carla Pobst had also caught the attention of the Rev. Youngun. With those three wild children of his, Laura wasn't sure if he'd ever find a wife.

True to his word, Rev. Youngun started it off with, "Wake up, the service is over."

Announcements were made about the upcoming Independence Day parade and picnic, with all the contests, the events, and the dance. They had a special event planned this year. The first annual children's horse race was announced, with a ten-dollar prize for the winner. All the kids began looking at one another, asking their parents if they could borrow the family horse for the race.

Rev. Youngun said, "Remember, children, ten dollars will buy a lot of schoolbooks."

While the older ladies nodded in agreement, the kids just snickered.

Terry Youngun looked at his brother Larry and whispered, "Ten bucks could buy all the candy in town!"

Only William "Silly Willy" Bentley, Jr., had his own horse. He sat gloating in his seat. The Youngun kids just looked at one another. Their pa was a minister, not a farmer. All they had was a mule named Crab Apple, who was slower than their spotted mutt, Dangit, and twice as mean as a stepped-on snake.

Rev. Youngun then announced that the traveling minister had fallen ill but that there was a substitute: Laura Ingalls Wilder would speak. Manly winked at her from the side of the room.

Laura smiled, bowed her head, and walked to the front of the room. Looking out over the faces of her friends and neighbors, she fought back the butterflies and began.

"While driving to church today, I passed a worn-out farm. Deep gullies were cut through the fields where the dirt had been washed away by the rains.

"The creek had been allowed to change its course in the bottom of the field and had cut out a new channel. It was ruining the good land in its way, taking the good dirt away, never to be brought back again."

She had the audience's attention, for protecting the land was dear to most farmers' hearts. "Tall weeds and brambles were taking more strength from the soil that was already so poor that grass would scarcely grow."

Pausing for effect and raising her voice, she began again. "As I viewed the place, I said to my husband, Manly, 'It's a crime! It is a crime to treat good land that way!' "

Throughout the audience heads nodded in agreement.

Looking directly at Bentley, Laura went on. "And just down from that ruined farm I saw where diseased trees had been cut down. I understand the trees needed to be cleared to keep the disease from spreading. That's just common sense."

Bentley thought she was complimenting him and nodded his head in thanks. Laura nodded back and looked directly at him. "It is all right to work and profit, but it is not all right to strip the forests and ruin the land. If trees are to be cut down, then new trees should be replanted. It just makes common sense!"

Bentley shook his head with a condescending smile.

But Laura was on a roll. "I will say it again. Whether it is the farmer who ruins his land or the logger who cuts down a tree without replanting another, it is a crime!"

Now the room was abuzz with excitement. Several people began nervously eyeing William Bentley, owner of the land in question.

Laura picked up the energy and increased her pace. "Yes, each of us 'inherits the earth' as the Bible says. But we only have the use of it while we live and must pass it on to those who come after us. We have no right to injure it or to lessen its value. To do so is dishonest. It's stealing from our children."

The audience began to applaud loudly. Rev. Youngun even

caught himself letting loose a short whistle. He didn't have to worry because his children were doing all the whistling he heard from the other side of the room.

William Bentley shook his head in disgust, put his hat on crooked, and stood up in a huff. Terry Youngun reached into his pocket and pulled out something green. Sarah Bentley adjusted her hat. A frog was croaking somewhere. She looked behind her at the Younguns. They smiled back at her with angelic faces.

As she stood up to leave, most of the church members began laughing. A big green bullfrog was sitting on the fruit on her hat, croaking merrily away.

"Silly Willy" Bentley, Jr., turned around and made an "I'll get you" face at Terry. He didn't see Larry's foot in front of him. "Silly Willy" looked pretty silly as he stumbled against his mother, who tumbled against her husband, who landed on his face. Then the frog switched hats and crawled into William Bentley's as he got up in a huff, dusted himself off, and about had a stroke when his hat jumped off his head!

Sherry suddenly screamed, "The hat's alive!"

Larry pulled his little sister back down into her seat. "Hush, you dummy! It's just Terry's frog under the hat!"

The whole church cracked up with laughter. Everyone enjoyed seeing the "high and mighty" Bentley brought down a peg or two. No one even noticed Terry Youngun picking up the frog and sticking it back into his pocket.

Laura hastily finished her speech to the applause of the still-laughing congregation and rejoined her family.

Old Man Bentley, the father of William, walked up to congratulate Laura. "Sounds like you're speaking about my boy William, Mrs. Wilder."

Laura didn't want any unpleasantness inside the church, so she laughed him off. "No, Mr. Bentley, I'm not singling out your son."

Old Man Bentley chuckled and shook his head. "No, I know you are, Mrs. Wilder. I know you are. I just hope he begins listenin' to you."

Laura's mouth opened. "You do?"

"Yup. I've tried to tell him that same thing, but he's been a stubborn cuss since he married that nasty woman from the East."

Old Man Bentley winked and walked off. He passed by Rev. Youngun, who had the young widow Carla Pobst by the arm, introducing her to the other ladies but not to the single men following behind her.

Laura was caught up in a crowd of well-wishers. When it was about over, Laura felt a tap on the shoulder and turned to see Andrew Jackson Summers, editor of the *Mansfield Monitor,* standing there. He claimed to be related to President Andrew Jackson, but most people just scoffed at that.

"I liked what I heard, Mrs. Wilder," said Summers, who was a big, rotund man. "Any chance you could write up your words for the *Mansfield Monitor?*"

Laura was taken aback. "Write it for the *Monitor?* I wasn't speaking from notes. I just made it up on the spot."

Summers smiled. "Take a stab at it, Mrs. Wilder. Those were powerful words."

Laura's butterflies were returning. "I appreciate your offer, but—"

Manly stepped up and took her arm. "But she can't have it to you until tomorrow."

Summers tipped his hat. "That will be fine. See you tomorrow, Mrs. Wilder."

When the editor was out of hearing range, Laura stamped her foot and looked her husband in the eye. "Manly, why did you promise him that?"

Manly put his arm around her. " 'Cause you've been writing in your diary for as long as I've known you. No telling what all you write about, but it's time you wrote for someone besides yourself."

Laura pushed his arm off. "Well, I may do it and I may not. It depends."

Manly eyed her closely. "Depends on what?"

Laura got a gleam in her eyes. "It depends on when I'm going to get my new telephone."

As an Oldsmobile sputtered by on the road out front, Manly turned. "And the next thing you'll be wanting will be a motor car."

Laura looked at the car driving away and said, "I just might, Manly Wilder. I just might."

Laura walked off singing "In My Merry Oldsmobile."

Rose came running over and hugged her mother. "Are we going to get a car, Momma?"

Manly slapped his forehead as they walked off. "Oh Lordy, why can't I just keep my mouth shut and leave well enough alone?"

CHAPTER 13

CRAB APPLE CAN DO IT!

As the Wilders drove back to Apple Hill Farm so Laura could work on her article for the *Mansfield Monitor*, the Youngun children were standing with their father outside the church. Their dog Dangit had waited faithfully for them and was nipping at Terry's pants' leg, eager to go home.

Rev. Youngun waved good-bye to the Wilders. "You children need to go right home and think about what you've learned in church today."

"Yes, Father," Larry and Sherry said. All Terry could think about was putting the frog on Mrs. Bentley's hat. That was what church should be like every Sunday!

Rev. Youngun looked down at his three children, "And I don't want you gettin' all excited about the horse race. You kids will just have to cheer on the others."

"Pa, why can't we enter the big race? Ten dollars is a lot of money," Larry said.

"Larry, you know we don't have a race horse."

"But we got your buggy horses and . . ."

Rev. Youngun interrupted him. "Son, those horses belong to the church. It wouldn't be right to use them for racing."

Terry piped up, "We've got Crab Apple the mule."

"Yeah," squawked Sherry, "Crab Apple can beat them all! Crab Apple can do it!"

Rev. Youngun smiled and shook his head. "Crab Apple's just an old mule, and mules are not known for their speed."

"Can we enter him, Father, can we?" Larry asked.

Rev. Youngun pushed them toward home. "If you can get Crab Apple to the starting line—much less the finish line— you can enter."

The children squealed with delight and headed home with Dangit yipping along beside them. Terry grabbed Larry's sleeve. "Crab Apple won't even walk fast to get food. He's never going to win that race."

Larry shrugged his shoulders, "Nothin' comes easy, Pa says. We'll just have to train him to be a race horse."

"How can a mule be a horse?" Sherry asked.

"Lunkhead," Terry exclaimed. "He didn't mean turn Crabbie into a horse."

"I don't understand," Sherry said, with a perplexed look on her face.

"Hush," Larry said, shutting one eye to think. "Where there's a will, there's a way . . . and there's got to be a way to get that mule to run fast and win that ten bucks."

"Good luck," Terry mumbled as they walked off together.

From behind them came Maurice Springer who was coming home from the African Methodist Episcopal church. "Mornin', Mr. Springer," they all said.

Maurice, who lived near the Younguns, knew that they'd gotten a wild streak in them ever since their momma had died from the fever. So he'd taken a kindly interest in them ever since.

"You children want a ride home?" Maurice asked, already knowing the answer. Before he could blink an eye, the three kids were scrambling up the side. "Ho, ho, hold on, don't rock the wagon, there's plenty of room for you all."

"What 'bout Dangit?" Sherry asked, looking down at the waggling, wiggling mutt.

"He can come along, too, if he don't nip at me again," Maurice said.

Dangit hopped in the back. Terry patted him on the head and said to Maurice, "Just don't use his name when you ain't callin' him, that's all he asks."

"Asks?" Maurice laughed. "That dog been speakin' to you?"

Dangit growled playfully. "I think he's speaking to you, Mr. Springer," Larry said.

"You heard about the big race?" Sherry asked.

Maurice nodded his head. "You mean the one with the ten dollar prize? I sure have. That's a lot of money for some young child to have."

"You know how to make a mule run, Mr. Springer?" Terry asked.

Maurice pulled his head back and looked at Terry. "Dangit, you trying to pull a joke on me, son?" Dangit growled from the back.

Terry bopped the mutt on the head. "Quiet, dog!"

"You can't make a mule run if it don't want to," Maurice said.

"But Mr. Springer," Larry said, "we don't have a horse to enter in the race . . ."

"Yeah," interrupted Sherry. "All we gots is Crab Apple the mule."

Maurice knew their dilemma but didn't have a real answer at first. Then he said, "Children, most mules I know are scared of hornets. They always run away from hornets."

"Everybody runs from hornets," Larry said.

"That's what I'm tellin' you. Put some hornets around that mule, and he'll run for glory."

Terry scratched his head, thinking about what Maurice had said. "Mr. Springer, what's the runningest mule you ever saw?"

Maurice shook the reins to help his slow-moving horses along. "Well, my daddy used to say if it's a white mule they don't run fast at all. But a black mule, why, he told me about one called Black Lightnin' that was so fast it ran over Monday, killed Tuesday, sen' ol' Wednesday to the hospital, crippled up Thursday, and told Friday to tell Saturday to be at the funeral home on Sunday."

"What happened to Black Lightnin'?" asked Larry.

"Why, he's still runnin' across the sky. You can hear the thunder of his hooves on the nights that it's so dark the raindrops come knockin' on your door askin' for a light to see where the ground is."

The Younguns started laughing. Maurice saw that they were about to pass a cemetery and turned his head away from them. "You children know that you're supposed to hold your breath when you pass a graveyard?"

They all shook their heads no. "Why, Mr. Springer?" Sherry questioned.

Maurice spun back around with his mouth wide open like a werewolf. " 'Cause if you don't, you'll be the next to die!"

He pointed a finger to the graveyard, and the three Younguns held their breaths with deep gulps. While the children turned from white to pink to red and blue, Dangit howled in fear.

At the end of the graveyard, the three Younguns expelled loudly. "Thought I was goin' to have to hold my breath until I was dead and buried," Larry exclaimed.

Sherry asked, out-of-breath, "Are those dead people still holdin' their breaths?"

"Nope," Maurice said. "Once you're dead, you're dead for all eternity," Maurice laughed.

"For all eternity?" asked Larry.

"That's right," Maurice said.

"How long's eternity, Mr. Springer?" Sherry asked.

Somewhat taken aback at such a big question from a small youngster, Maurice had to think about that for a moment. A rabbit dashed across the road in front of the wagon and gave Maurice an idea.

"You want to know how long eternity is? Well, let me explain it like this. Suppose that rabbit that just hopped across the road was to go to the Gulf of Mexico and fill his mouth with water. Then suppose he hopped to the beginning of the Mississippi River and spit it out. Then suppose he hopped back to the Gulf of Mexico to begin the drinkin' and spittin' again."

Sherry was nodding along as if what he was saying was something she had known all along.

"If he kept that drinkin', hoppin', and spittin' 'til the Gulf of Mexico was bone dry, why it wouldn't even be morning in eternity," Maurice said, smiling broadly.

"I don't like talkin' about graveyards and dead people," Terry shivered.

"Yeah," said Larry. "Let's talk about gettin' Crab Apple to run fast."

Sherry looked at the graveyard and started sniveling. "I don't want to die, Mr. Springer!"

"Look child, everyone's goin' to die."

"Even you?" she asked.

"Even me," nodded Maurice.

Sherry thought for a moment. "When I die, I want to spend eternity with you, Mr. Springer." She reached over and held his hand.

Maurice looked down at the tiny white hand almost hidden inside his big gnarled black hand. "I'll be there, child. Don't you worry. Maurice Springer will be sittin' there in eternity, waitin' for you."

Sherry rested her head against his side and closed her eyes. She loved Maurice. They all did.

Terry, never one for too much sentiment, whispered to Larry, "Too bad she ain't ready to check out now. I'm tired of sharin' my candy stash with her."

"That's not nice," Larry scolded.

"But it's the truth," Terry shrugged, thinking about all the extra candy he'd have if Sherry wasn't around.

CHAPTER 14

JUST BUSINESS

William Bentley stopped his buggy on the crest of the hill. Looking down at Mansfield, he was completely oblivious to the beauty of the surrounding countryside. His wife Sarah watched with concern, and his son Willy knew enough to stay out of his father's way when he got into one of his brooding moods.

Bentley was filled with rage over Laura's speech, grinding his teeth in anger. Sarah looked over with concern. "Don't let that Wilder woman bother you, William. She's just jealous."

"She embarrassed me at my church," Bentley said, shaking his head.

Sarah took his hand and rubbed it. "I'm sure they're going to make you a deacon. Those that give more money than others get selected first."

Willy asked from the back of the buggy, "How much does it cost to be a deacon, Father?"

Bentley shook his head. "That's not how it's supposed to be done, but that's how it is done!"

Willy shrugged his shoulders, a perplexed look on his face. "I don't understand. Can you buy your way into heaven?"

His mother turned and giggled. "Oh, Willy, that's a foolish thing to ask."

Bentley turned and winked at his son. "Everything's for sale in this life, and everybody has their price."

Willy was still confused. "What about the Golden Rule?"

His father cracked the whip over the horses. "There's only one rule—he who has the gold rules!"

Bentley guided the buggy down the hill and stopped next to the field of stumps at his last clearing operation. A pile of logs was set to be pulled to the railroad tracks, Bentley's brand on the end of each one.

In the same way that cowboys branded their cattle, timber barons like Bentley marked their ownership with log marks. A log without a brand was like an unmarked cow—anybody could claim it. Lumber rustlers would even hack off brands at intentionally created river logjams, so hired guns were employed throughout the country to protect the owners' property.

"Willy, you see that mark?" Bentley asked his son, pointing to the nearest log.

"Yes, Father."

"That circle B brand stands for your family's name." Sweeping his hand across a field of stumps, Bentley said, "One day this will be yours."

"What will I do with stumps, Father?"

Bentley rolled his eyes. "No, no, no! Not the stumps, the logging operation! We cut down some trees to save other trees and then sell the lumber to make money. That Wilder woman doesn't understand that if we leave diseased trees standing, the fungus will spread and kill all the trees in the Ozarks."

Willy looked at the field of stumps. "What'd she mean about your not replanting?"

Bentley turned to his son. "The county contract only calls for cutting 'em down. If they want the stumps cleared and trees replanted, then let 'em pay for it. There's more trees in America than we know what to do with."

Willy shook his head. "Stumps aren't even fun to play on. Who wants this kind of land?"

"Son," Bentley said, "that's not our problem. We get paid to do a job and make a profit to take care of ourselves. This is business, just business."

Two men—one white, one black—emerged from a row of uncut trees on top of the hill. Bentley blocked the sun with his arm to get a better view. "Those men are certainly hard workers," he said, pointing toward the two coming down the hill toward them.

"Who, dear?" Sarah asked.

"Flannigan and Carver. Can you imagine them working on Sunday?" Bentley shook his head at the loyalty of his workers.

John Flannigan was Irish, and Bentley's timber operations employed many of the men from the Hardacres, a section outside of Mansfield where the Irish families had congregated. These settlers had laid down roots in Missouri after escaping the Irish potato famine of 1845.

Jake Carver was a black drifter who had come with a "recommend" from a logging boss in Oregon.

"Hello, Mr. Bentley," Flannigan called out.

"Mornin'," added Carver, tipping his hat and nodding his head when they stood next to the buggy.

"Morning, boys," Bentley said proudly. "I'm surprised to see you working on Sunday. Don't you ever take a day off? Or do you think I'll pay you double for working on the Sabbath?" he chuckled.

"No, sir!" said Carver. "We were just up here looking at the fungus. Looks like it's spreading to that stand of twenty or thirty acres over yonder," he said, pointing to the woods they'd just come from.

"He's right, boss," said Flannigan. "Some of the trees about a hundred yards inside are dropping leaves. You'd better contact the county before it spreads across the next ridge."

Bentley took off his hat. "This fungus—or whatever it is— is sure a strange curse 'round here."

Carver nodded agreement. "Yes, sir. We had the same problem in Oregon. Took us almost two years to cut all the sick trees down."

Flannigan laughed. "Well, Mr. Bentley, what's bad for the trees is good for us. Keeps the lads in the Hardacres working, doesn't it?"

"Well," said Bentley, "tomorrow you bring in the marked boundaries of where we need to cut, and I'll get it to the powers that be in the county to get up a contract for the work."

"You'll have it in the mornin'," said Flannigan.

"Good," Bentley said, tightening the buggy reins. "You two need to take the rest of the day off. You've done enough to help the company this day."

The two men waved as the Bentleys drove off.

Flannigan looked at Carver. "That man should be givin' us a raise for all we're doin' for the company."

Carver chuckled. "He just don't know how valuable we are to his company—yet."

CHAPTER 15

WHY DO YOU KEEP COWS?

Laura had stayed up most of the night writing and re-writing her article for Mr. Summers's newspaper and had fallen asleep at the table. Her article was titled "We Are the Heirs of the Ages."

Manly had told her to mention William Bentley by name and be hard on him, but Laura felt she was writing about more than just William Bentley and his wasteful timber-cutting practices.

In her diary she had written: *"There are ruined farms all over the county. All over the state. You don't have to be rich to be ignorant and wasteful. There are a lot of Bentleys out there."*

Manly shouted from the kitchen. "Come here, Laura, I've got a present for you."

Laura smiled, puzzled at what Manly could have.

Manly had his head in the Puritan icebox that he had bought her from the Sears catalog after the last harvest. His fingers were drumming on the solid brass hinges as he stared at the contents of the icebox.

The top of the icebox served as a kind of sideboard shelf

and had plates of meat, cheese, and butter already sitting upon it. Laura looked at the array of food and shook her head. "You better close that door before all the ice melts."

Manly pulled his head out and turned. "Just trying to make myself a sandwich, Laura. My stomach is growling."

Laura giggled. "It's probably growling that it's still stuffed from the breakfast for three you ate this morning. What have you got for me?"

Manly stood up, smiling. "Take a guess."

Laura got a little-girl look on her face. "I know, a 'ring-ring hello-hello.'"

Manly frowned. "A what?"

"A telephone."

He shook his head. "No, it's not a telephone. I'm working on getting that for you, but there aren't any phone lines near the farm. I got you something you can really use." He smiled, pointing to an odd shape sticking up under a sheet on the floor. "You're going to like it."

"It's not a book," she said, suspiciously eyeing the covered object.

"Nope, it's not a book, girl," he guffawed.

Laura walked over for a closer inspection. "Is it something for the car I want?"

Manly was flustered. "Lands, no! It's got nothing to do with a car! It's something you really need."

"Manly, are you just trying to butter me up? Are you up to something?"

Manly laughed. "You might say I'm trying to butter you up." He pulled the sheet off. "This here's the present. Now throw away that old dash butter churn. This churn will bring in the butter in three minutes!"

A new churn? That was the last thing in the world she wanted!

"That's very kind of you, Manly, but—"

Manly waved his arm over the churn as if it were a pile of gold. "But what? The Sears salesman found out we didn't have a new-style churn and asked me, 'Buddy, what do you keep cows for?' I said, 'To make money.' Well, he proceeded to tell me that dairying is one of this country's most important farm industries and is becoming more important every day and—"

"Excuse me for interrupting you, but Apple Hill is not a dairy farm."

Manly didn't miss a beat. "That don't matter, the Sears man told me. We keep our cow for milk, and the most valuable part of milk is the butterfat."

"So?"

Manly arched his eyebrows. "So? You can make us some extra money by making butter to sell and skimming the milk better."

Laura covered the churn back up. "But we just make butter for ourselves nowadays. The farm crops are what we sell."

Manly pulled the cover right back off. "We've got to modernize, Laura Ingalls Wilder. There's nothing but waste and work for you and me, using the old churn."

She picked the sheet back up. "What's this 'you and me using the old churn'? How would you know? You've never used it." With a twirl of her wrists, she covered the churn back up.

Manly scuffed his feet and pulled the cover back off again. He had the old hurt, puppy-dog look in his eyes. "I was just thinking about you, Laura."

Laura said facetiously, "Thanks, Manly. Thanks for think-ing about what I really need."

Having missed entirely the annoyance in her voice, Manly was now quite satisfied with himself. He took his sandwich and Laura's newspaper article and walked toward the barn, whistling.

While Manly rode to town to deliver her article to Sum-mers at the newspaper, Laura played around with the new churn, cutting her hands on the sharp tin paddles.

When Manly returned, he told her how Andrew Jackson Summers was waiting at the door for him and took her article right to press.

"That man's office is such a mess. Don't see how he gets the paper out with all the junk lying around." Seeing that Laura had been using his gift, he asked, "How'd the churn work out, Buttercup? Aren't you excited?"

Laura was none too pleased. "I wish you'd bring in my old dash churn. It's much easier to use than this contraption." Eyeing it suspiciously, she asked, "Are you sure that two people aren't supposed to operate this thing?"

Tossing back his head with a laugh, Manly said, "No, the man said it was a one-woman show."

"More like a circus sideshow," Laura mumbled.

"What? I missed that," Manly said, opening the icebox door to look for a snack.

Laura pushed the churn away from her, but it teetered back and forth until it landed back against her leg. Shaking her head in disgust, she looked toward Manly, who was al-ready eating something. "Oh, nothing. Yes, you're right, this new patent churn is something else."

Manly burped. " 'Scuse me." He looked at the churn and

said, "It's something else. You bet it is. Why, you can churn in three minutes with this. The old one took 'bout half a day."

Laura ignored the fact that, like most men lecturing about home economics, he didn't know what he was talking about. "Manly, it's just too hard to hold down and turn at the same time."

Manly picked up the churn and fiddled with it like the expert he wasn't. "Just put one end of a board on the churn and the other on a chair and sit on the board. That way you can hold the churn down easy!" He set it down and headed back toward the icebox.

When Manly looked the other way, Laura gave the churn a kick. "Kind of like a housewife's rodeo, Manly?" The churn fell over with a loud crash.

"Huh?" said Manly, turning around. "What happened?"

Laura picked it up. "I told you, the doggone thing's just unstable." She walked over and put her hands on Manly's shoulder. "Manly, I just wish you'd bring in my old dash churn."

Manly shook his head, licking a piece of pie from his lower lip. "I put it away, way up in the barn."

Laura lifted the paddles from the churn and held the sharp objects for his inspection. "Please bring it. These churn paddles cut my hands when I try to wash them."

"Oh pshaw, woman! I got you a churn that brings butter in three minutes. Just soak those paddles and use a rag to hold 'em so you won't cut your hands."

Manly walked out the kitchen door. In a minute, he was back, handing Laura a board. When he left, Laura tried again. She put the board on top of the churn and sat on it as if she were riding a horse.

She laughed out loud. "I wonder if this is how they churn butter in Texas!"

CHAPTER 16

STUBBORN AS A MULE

Wile Laura was riding her churn, all the farm kids in the county were practicing for the big race. Only Silly Willy Bentley had a riding horse of his own. He'd prance through town on his new saddle, wearing a silk jockey suit that his mother had tailored for him, looking like a sausage stuffed in a silk casing sitting on a big bun.

The rest of the kids were busy trying to convert their parents' plow, pack, and team horses to their image of Kentucky Derby winners. Took a lot of imagination, but that's one thing most kids have.

The Younguns looked as if they'd been in a fight. They had bruises, black eyes, and enough sticker-bush cuts to look like battle-hardened soldiers. Crab Apple the mule just didn't want any part of being a racehorse. If he could have talked, he would have said, "You can't make a mule into a horse." But of course mules can't talk, and the Younguns probably wouldn't have listened to Crab Apple anyway.

After all, he was just a mule.

On Sunday afternoon, their Pa had told them he was going to work on a sermon he was planning to give to the

Rotary Club, and he wanted things quiet. The Younguns, being Younguns, played a Bible game their own way.

Larry said, "Let's play Noah's Ark, and I'm Noah."

"Noah's Ark?" asked Terry. "What's that?"

"Well," Larry said, taking the role of big brother, "Pa said to talk about Bible stories, so let's try and re-create the story of Noah's Ark." Larry looked over at their ornery mule. Crab Apple blinked an eye and turned his head, trying to figure what those fool kids were up to now. Pointing to Crab Apple with a flourish, Larry said, "The first animal that Noah wants brought on board is a mule with a saddle on."

Terry looked at Sherry, who shrugged her shoulders. "The Bible don't say nothin' about Noah wantin' a mule," Terry said.

"Noah wanted two of every animal so they could add and multiply their own kind," Larry responded, trying to sound like a biblical authority.

"Mr. Springer said mules don't have babies," said Terry, slowly shaking his head. "And who'd want two Crab Apples, anyway?"

"Yeah, one's bad 'nough," agreed Sherry.

Larry went ahead with the Bible game, and they pulled out the old saddle. Crab Apple eyed it suspiciously. When they tried to put the saddle on old Crab Apple, he kicked and knocked a hole through the barn door. They kept trying to saddle him until they finally gave up and decided to ride the wild mule Indian-style, with just a blanket.

Crab Apple seemed taller than the three Younguns combined, so they got a short ladder from the shed and stood in line to climb on. Only Crab Apple didn't understand the procedure, and every time Larry whispered "ready," Crab Apple moved forward just as one of them stepped off the ladder.

After landing in the mud, dust, and fresh meadow muffins that Crab Apple kept dropping, they finally got the idea to blindfold the critter. Larry wrapped a towel around his head, and Crab Apple calmed down.

"I'm first!" shouted Terry.

"No, me first!" screamed Sherry.

Larry put his hands between them both. "No, here's how we'll decide."

> Enie-meanie-minie-mo,
> Catch a heathen by the toe,
> If he hollers make him pay,
> Fifty dollars every day.

When he stopped, he was pointing to himself. "I'm first."

"The heathen's the first to get on," Terry wisecracked.

Larry wasn't a heathen, but he wanted to get started so he got on. When all three were finally on his back, Crab Apple took off and ran as if the devil was after him. Dangit woke up from his nap under the front porch and barked along behind them, thinking it was a game.

"Stop, Crab Apple! Stop!" Larry and Terry screamed.

Their father was sitting in the living room working on a sermon and looked up, but Crab Apple had already dashed past, carrying his three scared riders. Rev. Youngun came out on the porch when Crab Apple kicked another hole in the barn door, but seeing nothing—Crab Apple was running through the creek like a deer by then—he went back inside.

Sherry just hung on and closed her eyes as the mule ran right in front of a honking motor car.

They all screamed as the car came within inches of hitting them. The driver honked, shaking his fist at them.

Crab Apple jumped fences and ditches, ran through the woods and brambles. It was a regular Paul Revere's ride through the countryside until he kicked up a skunk who sprayed them all with stink juice.

Dangit began rolling around in the dirt and tore through the creek, trying to get the stink juice off. The Younguns couldn't hold their noses because they were holding on for dear life.

Rev. Youngun looked up briefly as Crab Apple passed the window again, but again, he was too slow to see the cause of all the commotion. He did notice a funny odor, though. "I hope the outhouse isn't overflowing again," he mumbled to himself.

For the Younguns, the worst was yet to come. Their black neighbor and friend Maurice Springer had seen most of their ride from a distance and now took a ringside seat on the split-rail fence. When they raced past him, he held his nose and burst out laughing. "Phewee," he called after them, "you kids stink something fierce!"

Crab Apple went kicking through the neighbor lady's laundry, got tangled in the lines, and pulled her clothes through the mud. She came out screaming, waving her broom at them, but she stopped when Crab Apple aimed a kick in her direction. Maurice began shaking his head—a three-Youngun wupping was soon coming.

With a laundry sheet wrapped tight around them all, Crab Apple blindly raced down the road. He ran past a family of

French Canadians, who thought they'd seen a ghost and began praying as fast as they could.

"Smelly ghosts," said the father.

"The devil's smell," added the mother, holding her nose and still praying.

Maurice howled with laughter. "That smelly ghost is about as welcome as passin' wind in church!"

Sherry would have prayed, but she couldn't put her hands together. They were held vise-grip tight on the back of Terry . . . who was holding Larry's belt loops even tighter.

Larry was holding onto Crab Apple's ears, and when they bumped into a low-hanging hornets' nest, several flew under the sheet and stung the mule. Crab Apple took off and raced like greased lighting.

Maurice laughed so hard that he thought he'd split a gut or worse. "That mule can run. Boy, *that mule can run!* Silly Willy better watch out. Hornets will make anything run fast!"

Crab Apple shook the sheet off his head, saw the hornets after him, and galloped back to the barn. At the edge of the corral he stopped dead in his tracks, only Larry, Terry, and Sherry didn't stop. They kept on flying through the air, right into the mud puddle in the center of the pigpen.

Dangit and the fat old pig sat at the edge of the mud puddle, looking at the mud-covered, stinky kids. Standing next to the barn was their father, inspecting the holes that Crab Apple had kicked in the door. "So the three little pigs were reflecting on the Bible, were they?" He looked at his children and raised his arm. "Larry, Terry, and Sherry, come here! March!"

The pig grunted, "Oink-oink." He was probably glad these

three messy kids were leaving his bathtub. What with the mud and the dust and the fresh meadow muffin that Terry had landed in, their father was fit to be tied. It was not like him to spank the kids, but he wasn't a rod sparer, either.

Larry looked at Terry, who looked at Sherry and whispered, "Get ready to cry."

After calming down the neighbor lady and handing her back the muddy skunk sheet that the pigs had taken a liking to, Pa scolded them all. "If your mother were here, she'd know what to do. I asked you to reflect on the Bible, and you three children go gallivantin' around the countryside like Ichabod Crane. What do you have to say for yourselves?"

Rev. Youngun stood before them with that "wuppin' " look in his eyes. Larry nudged Terry who gave Sherry a quick elbow in the ribs. Sherry began to cry . . . and cry and cry and cry—which always made their father feel weak. It loosened his resolve and made him more likely to spare the rod on their behinds, which were already hurting at the thought of a belt wuppin'.

Sherry's crying worked almost every time. "Don't hit us, Pa. Please don't hit us," they all said in unison. Sherry ran up and grabbed his leg, crying. "I miss my momma."

Caught off guard, he stammered, "Well . . . er . . ." and then closed his eyes. "Lord, give me guidance in dealing with my children."

"Amen," the children said on cue.

Rev. Youngun opened his eyes and looked suspiciously at his children. "Is there anything you children want to say before judgment is given?"

The crying hadn't worked! The three children stared at the belt he was preparing to take off.

Larry got an inspiration and whispered, "Pa, Proverbs says, 'An angry father makes foolish mistakes.' "

Rev. Youngun was always surprised when his children popped out Bible verses at exactly the right moment. "No, it says, 'He that is soon angry dealeth foolishly.' "

Larry didn't miss a cue. "A father is a 'he,' ain't he, Pa?"

Terry jumped in before their father could answer. "And Matthew says, 'For if you forgive your children their trespasses, your God will also forgive your Pa.' "

Rev. Youngun shook his head, "No, it says if you forgive 'men,' not children, their—"

It was Larry's turn. "But all men are God's children, aren't they, Pa?"

"Hallelujah," added Sherry, looking up from where she was wrapped around her father's leg.

Rev. Youngun had lost again, and he knew it. What was the use? How could you whip children who loved their Bible so? "Okay, okay. Pile your dirty clothes behind the barn so I can burn 'em—then head down to the creek with some lye soap."

"You mean skinny-dip, Pa?" Terry asked.

"Me, too, Pa?" Sherry asked.

Closing his eyes, wishing that his wife Norma was still there to handle such things, he looked upward and said quietly, "Norma, help me. Give me guidance."

He paused as if hearing an answer, then looked at his three smelly, scratched-up, mud-and-manure-covered children. "You all smell like you're skunk dipped. Sherry, you keep your underbritches on 'til I bring you all towels. But we've got to bury those clothes. Go on. Get that smell off you."

As they ran like two and a half naked jaybirds toward the creek, Rev. Youngun shook his head. "I'm never going to find another momma for these wild monkeys."

Maurice walked off mumbling to himself, "That mule can run, boy! That mule can run!"

CHAPTER 17

FOOD FOR THOUGHT

It was the big day. Laura's first newspaper article was going to be published, and like any new author, she was a nervous wreck. Rose was off visiting friends, so the only way Laura knew how to get her mind off things was to eat—and eat she did.

She was so nervous thinking about seeing her name in print, she made two dozen doughnuts to dip in powdered sugar. Manly watched her fingers form and twist the raised doughnut circles, then just as quickly drop them into the boiling lard.

He stood back because he didn't want any of the hot fat jumping out on him. The kitchen table was covered with flour, baking soda, and powdered sugar, and when the doughnuts were hot and ready, Manly burned his mouth trying to eat the first one too quickly.

Laura put a half-dozen in a sack and sent Manly into town to get a copy of the paper. The Sears "wish book" was open to the corset section. She quickly closed it. The last thing she wanted to think about was holding in her tummy. All she wanted to think about was food!

Manly went speeding toward town without noticing the newly posted ten-mile-per-hour speed signs. He came barreling as fast as he pleased right inside the city limits.

Parking his wagon in front of the newspaper office, Manly was about to jump off and go get the paper when he felt a tap on the shoulder. It was Sheriff Peterson, the Swede who had been elected sheriff because he was the biggest man in the county.

"Hi, Sheriff. You catchin' any lawbreakers today?" Manly asked politely, hoping the sheriff would just pass him by.

"Yup," the big Swede said, seeming in no hurry to move along. As Manly stepped to the side, the sheriff stepped in front of him.

"Something you need, Sheriff?" Manly asked, stepping to the other side.

"Yup," said the sheriff.

Manly was in a hurry and didn't want to get in a long, drawn-out conversation with the lawman.

" 'Scuse me, Sheriff, but I'm kind of in a hurry."

Peterson pulled out his new pad of speeding tickets. "I noticed."

"You noticed what?"

"I noticed that you didn't notice the speed-limit signs. You were a goin' at least twenty miles an hour." He looked down and began writing. "Sorry, Manly, but I've got to give you a ticket."

Manly slapped his leg, "A ticket! Speed limits are for motor cars, not for wagons. Any fool knows that!" The sheriff kept writing, but Manly was hot under the collar. "I said, any fool knows that!"

The sheriff looked up. "Well, this fool knows the law is the law. If you go over ten miles an hour in this town, it don't matter whether you're ridin' a horse or drivin' a motor car. I'm going to give you a ticket."

With that, he handed Manly the fifty-cent speeding ticket and walked off. Manly just stood there, dumbfounded.

From behind him came a familiar voice. "Got you too, I see." It was Dr. George, Mansfield's only doctor, who just happened to be the only doctor in the county. Everybody loved and respected the black man, who'd delivered most of the babies around.

"Oh, hi, Doc," Manly said, tossing the ticket onto the floorboard of the wagon. "That's the silliest thing I ever heard, givin' speedin' tickets to wagons. I never thought he was a blockhead, but maybe folks are right."

Dr. George shook his head. "Just 'cause one out of every five Swedes in the world lives in America, don't give cause to call 'em all blockheads."

Manly smiled. "Shucks, Doc, I wasn't callin' 'em all block-heads, just this one."

Dr. George grinned. "Well, you know how the sheriff is. If the law said the moon was made out of green cheese and he had to get him some for lunch, that man would spend the rest of his days tryin' to figure out how to get up there!" They both laughed. "That's a good article by your wife."

Manly brightened up. "You've seen it?"

"Seen it? Everyone is talking about it. Word of her facing down Bentley at church is all over the county."

Manly picked up a paper from the stack on the sidewalk, leaving a penny in the box. He looked and looked through the pages. Dr. George patiently watched him, then pointed to the article. Manly beamed with joy when he saw "By Laura Ingalls Wilder" under the title.

As Dr. George walked off, he said over his shoulder, "You tell Laura to do like President T. R. Roosevelt says, and 'walk softly but carry a big stick.' "

"Why tell her that?"

" 'Cause Bentley's not a man to be fooled with lightly," the doctor said, ambling off up the street.

Manly stood there, watching the doctor walk off, thinking about what he had just said. Feeling a tap on his shoulder from behind, Manly turned. It was Chan, who owned the Chinese Store, which was a peculiar institution to prairie and rural towns. Chan's store sold tea, canned fish, strange dried foods, and firecrackers for the kids. Chan took in laundry on the side. Like most businesses in Mansfield, Chan's store offered a lot of different things.

Chan's family had come to America from China to build the rail lines across America and had never gone back. People thought he looked strange with his long black shirt and ponytail hanging down his back, but Chan was a nice man who lived quietly with his wife and son.

Manly smiled. "Oh, hi, Mr. Chan. How are you today?"

Chan nodded his head up and down. "Very good, Manly, very good. I am most pleased with your wife's article."

Knowing how Chan could talk when he got the urge, Manly began trying to disengage from the conversation and get back up on the wagon. "I'll tell Laura what you said, Mr. Chan. She'll be pleased."

"Ah, Manly, perhaps your wife would be so kind as to want to write about my story. About my Grandfather Wing We Wo. He . . ."

"Mr. Chan, I'm kind of in a hurry and—"

Chan nodded his head. "This will only take one minute." Being too polite to escape, Manly sat there patiently. Chan began: "My Grandfather Wing We Wo was very, very wealthy and fat and wore a red and yellow girdle. He never worked a day in his life and had long, long fingernails to prove it. Every day he ate bird's nest soup with shark's fins and deer's sinews and . . ."

Two hours later, Manly walked into the kitchen. He handed Laura the paper and said, "Don't ever mention bird's nest soup to me!"

"What?" she asked, looking perplexed.

CHAPTER 18

THE OTHER SIDE OF TOWN

On the other side of town, Sarah Bentley was sitting in her fancy parlor reading about life in New York—about the parties, the opera, and all the other events she missed in Mansfield.

She sat back and sighed to herself. "There's no place like New York!"

That wasn't how most people west of Manhattan felt about the place. Manly thought that Bat Masterson had been right when he called New York "an unfinished mining camp."

Laura had read an anonymous description that she felt hit the target: "A mile-high wall of sad people to be ascended by social climbers plunging their knives into the backs of others and pulling themselves up by any means possible."

To Sarah Bentley, New York was the center of the earth. There was no other place to live—unless you married for money. Then you could end up anyplace . . . like Mansfield, Missouri.

When she had been introduced to her future husband during his first and last business trip to New York, it had been love at first sight. Her mother said he was "a rich timber man from the South," so Sarah immediately set her sights on being the queen of his plantation.

William didn't own a sprawling plantation with dozens of servants at his every beck and call and didn't attend the society functions each year in Charleston, South Carolina. However, like all self-important men, he knew how to tell a good tale.

When Sarah bragged about life in New York, William just said, "In Mansfield, everything is dignified, prettier than any-place else in the whole world. Why, from my home you can look out and see our Ozark land for miles and miles around."

Of course Sarah thought that he must have the biggest plantation around, and she did everything except put out a bear trap to catch him. And catch him she did.

William thought she had money, and since he wanted to marry money, he was an easy catch. She was pretty and had family connections, so with him being a young man on the way up, they were a good match.

Leaving New York after a swirl of wedding parties, Sarah sat on the train with her new husband and talked about what her new life would be like. "Do the ladies of Mansfield wear walking skirts or peek-a-boo shirtwaists when they stroll down the main boulevard during the evening after the op-era?"

Not daring to look her in the face, he said, "Oh, they wear some skirts and dresses, they do."

He didn't say what kind of skirts. What *would* Sarah say when she saw some of the local women wearing dresses or overalls and pulling plows in the fields?

Touching the hat she had ordered from the exclusive ladies fashion magazine, *L'Art de la Mode and le Charme United,* Sarah asked, "Are their hats the toques with satin bows or egret plume hats with satin-faced brims?"

"Oh, they wear hats, they do," William responded, keeping his nose in the newspaper.

Sarah said playfully, "Put that newspaper down, silly. Are the hats two-toned or flowered silk?"

William remembered seeing the wife of one of his tenant farmers wearing a hat all splattered with manure after she was kicked by a mule. "Let's see. Most of the hats are two-toned."

"Oh, wonderful!" she exclaimed. She had over fifty hats in her collection and just knew she'd be the hit of Mansfield. "I'm sure it will be an experience comparing hats with the ladies of the town."

Bentley suppressed a laugh and put the newspaper in front of his face. "Sarah, you'll probably get a kick out of it. The local ladies do."

She asked a lot of questions about Mansfield on the train ride. When he told her that the people of Mansfield liked to imitate bird and animal cries, she thought it must be some kind of social affair to raise funds for the Audubon Society. Never in her wildest dreams did she imagine sitting around with neighbors having a wild-turkey-gobbling contest.

Nor could she conceive that "barking off squirrels" was not some kind of nature campaign. Later, when she saw that it was a contest to use a black powder rifle and shoot the bark off just under a squirrel so that the concussion would kill the creature, she was appalled.

When an old Ozark man brought her a plate of cooked

squirrel heads for her to "eat the tongue and slurp down the brains," Sarah fainted dead away!

On her arrival in Mansfield, Sarah saw a town smaller than the block around her house in New York. There were no skyscrapers, no trolleys, no automobiles—just a dirt main street with country folk going about their business. There would be no strolling after the opera, because there wasn't an opera . . . or playhouse, summer band shell, or fine restaurant.

Welcome to Mansfield, Missouri.

CHAPTER 19

JOB INSURANCE

John Flannigan leaned against the tree, watching Jake Carver working the hand drill. "Jake, where'd you learn this trick?"

Carver laughed. "Man named Clive Thompson, the boss out in Grants Pass, Oregon. He showed me how to keep the work goin'."

Flannigan stood up and took his turn with the drill. The base of the tree had a ring of virtually invisible holes around the base. "How long were you able to keep it up?"

"Worked for almost two years," Carver said, taking a sip of whiskey from the jug.

"Two years? Why'd you stop? Did you run out of trees?" Flannigan laughed.

Carver wiped his lips. "Naw, it'd be still goin' on if the boss hadn't asked someone else to fix the trees when I broke my arm. Can't trust nobody nowadays."

"Whatta you think Bentley would do if he knew that it ain't fungus that's killin' the trees?" Flannigan asked.

Carver stood up and inspected the series of holes in the tree base. Each one was done at angles inside the natural folds in the the bark, to keep them hidden. "The man's a businessman. All he cares 'bout is money."

Flannigan counted the trees around them that they'd drilled this morning. "We've done thirty trees 'round here today alone."

Carver looked around. "By next week, people will think that the fungus has spread over here."

"We're makin' that man a lot of money. Don't seem fair that he ain't sharin' the wealth," Flannigan said coldly.

"I got a plan. I ain't working two years for my hourly pay."

"What've you got in mind, Jake?"

"I think that after the next county contract is issued, we should have a little talk with him about the job insurance we've been givin' for free. Time for him to start payin' the doctor."

The two men each took a long swig of the moonshine and picked up their tools. After about half a mile, Carver stopped and looked at the base of a tree they'd drilled a month before. Drops of sap, looking like watered-down molasses, were dripping slowly out. The leaves were yellowing on the ends of the upper branches.

"Looks like the fungus has hit here," Carver laughed.

"That poison you're spiking in sure does the trick," said Flannigan, shaking his head in admiration of the scam they were working.

"Worked in Oregon, and it works every time. Keeps us eatin' three squares a day and makin' it so's it ain't a long time between drinks."

"I'll drink to that," Flannigan said, and they hiked back toward the road.

CHAPTER 20

FREEDOM OF THE PRESS

Laura's articles began to appear regularly in the *Mansfield Monitor*. Some were reprinted in papers throughout the state. Manly had bought her a Kodak box camera, and Laura's pictures were also finding their way into print.

She attacked illiteracy, advocated women's right to vote, and preached self-confidence and not depending on the government to take care of you. Her words touched the soul of farm families and city merchants who were independent, caring Americans.

She opposed the *status quo* in many ways but was not like some journalists of the day who wanted to topple the system. Laura concentrated on the people and conditions of Wright County, Missouri. Protecting the land was her greatest concern. She had seen ruined farms and barren fields all across the prairies of America. She didn't want to see more of them here.

Laura took her latest column in hand, hitched up the buggy, and headed to town to deliver it herself. There was a shorter route, but Laura went by way of the logging areas.

She wanted to take pictures of Bentley's men at work, stripping the land without replanting for the future.

The men didn't recognize Laura as the journalist causing trouble and posed for pictures with their axes and saws in hand. Laura stood by the buggy, clicking her Kodak away, getting devastating pictures to go with her story. Thanking the men, she drove into town and almost rode into William Bentley, who was crossing the street to his office.

He began to tip his hat, but seeing who she was, he retracted it quickly. "Oh, it's you, Mrs. Wilder. For a moment I thought you were Mrs. Knutson, the world's most famous female bullwhacker."

Laura pulled her wagon to a stop. She never flinched from a verbal confrontation with a bully. "Oh, it's you, Mr. Bentley. For a moment I thought it was Paul Bunyan himself, but I didn't see Babe the blue ox! Which reminds me, how's Mrs. Bentley?"

Thinking he'd been insulted, but not quite sure, he answered carefully, "She's fine, Mrs. Wilder. Me, Paul Bunyan? I'm not quite that tall, Mrs. Wilder, but you sure do drive a buggy like a bullwhacker."

"Nothing wrong with bullwhackers, Mr. Bentley. They moved a lot of freight for homesteaders. 'Course the companies gave them Bibles as protection against moral contamination in case they ran over something." Nudging her wagon closer to Bentley, she added, "You know, something like a skunk in the road, maybe."

Bentley laughed. "I got to hand it to you, lady. You think like a man!"

"One's sex doesn't determine thinking ability, Mr. Bentley. A person either thinks or doesn't think . . . like yourself."

Bentley glared. "You're a hateful woman! I'm glad I don't have to wake up with you each morning."

Laura answered with a single, harsh laugh. "I can appreciate that," she said, looking him in the eye. "You've got more than your share to wake up to each morning as it is."

Bentley shook his finger at her. "You got a big mouth, woman—a real big mouth."

Starting the wagon forward, she called over her shoulder, "That's why we'll have the vote soon."

Bentley took his hat off and hit it against his leg. "No way you will!" As she drove away he mumbled to himself, "Dog-gone woman suffragist."

Laura turned the buggy around and rode toward Bentley again. He stood his ground as she drove directly toward him. The buggy came to a stop with the tip of the horse's nose almost touching Bentley's. The horse snorted in Bentley's face.

Laura looked at Bentley. "Women will have the vote. It's a part of progress that can't be stopped."

"Someone's been keepin' you in the dark, woman. Men will never let that come to be while the sun shines," he snapped back.

Laura's horse snorted again and gave Bentley a wet kiss. Laura laughed and said, "No one can hide the sun with their fingers. Not even you, Mr. Bentley—not even you."

Without another word, Laura turned the buggy and went up the street to the newspaper office. The confrontation had made Laura so angry that she banged open the door of the *Mansfield Monitor*.

"Well, hello, Laura. Nice of you to enter so quietly," said

Summers with a smile. His expression quickly changed when he saw the scowl on her face.

"That Bentley makes me so mad!"

"What happened now? You two get to debatin' on the street?"

"Let me cool off first," she said, putting her purse down.

She looked around the newspaper office. It was a sight to see. Alongside President Roosevelt's picture hung two country hams, a dirty shirt, a string of onions, and an odd assortment of past issues. The cookstove and heater took up most of the other wall. Over it hung engravings, a pair of boots, a bearskin, and a rifle.

"You ought to clean this place up," she said, without looking at Summers.

"Newspaper editin' is a man's world, Laura."

"So what else is new?" she said, picking up her pad.

As she began to write, Summers kept trying to read over her shoulders, but he finally got the hint that she wanted privacy when she said, "Do you mind?"

Finally, Laura put the pencil down and read what she had just written. It was time to draw the line and dare Mr. Bentley to cross over it.

THE WANTON DESTRUCTION OF TREES
By Laura Ingalls Wilder

Driving to town, I passed over a long stretch of the road where the large, beautiful native oaks and walnut trees had been cleared away. The land had been left bare and ugly by William Bentley's timber company.

Less than half a mile down the road, the loggers were stripping another patch bare. They kindly posed for pictures with their saws in hands, proud of the work they were getting paid to do.

"It's my job," one told me. "I do what I get paid to do."

Yes, it's their job, but who has the job of making sure our children will have forests to enjoy around Mansfield?

The timber company gets paid by the county to cut down the trees without any thought to replanting. Yes, I know they have a contract with the county to cull the acreage the fungus has spread to, but anyone with common sense would have the logging contract include replanting.

Is anyone in the county government listening? Cutting without replanting is a fool's game that we all lose!

Laura handed the article to Summers, who whistled as he read it. "Oh boy! He ain't gonna like this." He dropped the article on the table. "Laura Wilder, Bentley's going to go crazy over this."

"You think he'll like it that much?" she said playfully.

"No! I'll be lucky if those loggers of his don't burn the building down!"

Laura stood up. "It's important that we save trees if we can. You can't imagine what an endless prairie looks like without a tree in sight for miles."

"Do you know how many trees it takes to make the paper for just one edition of the *Mansfield Monitor?*"

"I know, and I don't care. That's not wasting trees," she huffed, turning to leave. "And besides," she said, looking back, "I'm sure your paper comes from loggers who replant."

"Don't be too sure about that. You'd never know if the paper came from Bentley's trees."

Laura left Summers shaking his head, knowing that a fight was coming. Though Bentley had money, Laura had the determination of a bulldog. Summers worried that everyone else around them would be the real losers.

When the paper came out the next morning, William Bentley was sitting in his elegant office reading aloud Laura's column. Slamming his fist down on the table, he picked up the phone. He turned the crank to get the Mansfield switchboard operator on the line.

A squeaky voice sounded. "This is Clara. Can I help you?"

"Clara, this is William Bentley. Get me Andy Summers on the line, will ya?"

Clara, who had few calls and a lot of time to chitchat and pass gossip, responded quickly.

"Yes, sir, Mr. Bentley, I'll ring him up right now. I just hope those darned buzzards haven't knocked the lines down again."

It took her a moment to connect the lines. "Summers, this is Bentley."

Andrew Jackson Summers was busy cooking up a rabbit with one hand and holding an Edgar Allan Poe book in the other. Hearing Bentley's voice, he sighed. "Yes, Mr. Bentley, what can I do for you?"

"You can stop printing that Wilder woman."

Summers had been expecting the call. It had been only a matter of time before a thin-skinned, wealthy blowhard like Bentley tried to exert pressure.

"Now, Mr. Bentley, there's such a thing as freedom of the press."

Bentley snorted. "And there's such a thing as having your loan called at the bank. Nothing's free in this world, Summers. Those presses of yours certainly weren't, and the bank's got the note to prove it."

Bentley stood up with the phone in his hand, staring through the window toward the newspaper office just down the street. Summers was staring back. There was silence on the line.

Bentley pointed his finger. "Do you understand me, Summers? Just 'cause the county won't appropriate enough money for replanting isn't my fault. And the spreading fungus isn't my fault."

Summers interrupted. "I'll think about what you're saying, Bentley. I'll think about it."

"You think about this. If I don't stop this darn fungus, then everyone will be blaming me for losing their orchards and shade trees. How about a little editorial understanding on your part, Mr. Editor?"

"As I said, I'll think about it." Andrew Jackson Summers hung up the phone. He didn't want to tell Laura or anyone about the call. He needed some time to think about it over lunch.

Clara the operator didn't have to think about it. When Bentley clicked off, she began crossing lines as fast as her hands could fly, spreading the word about Bentley's threat. By nightfall the story was all over the county—passed over fences and phone lines. Clara's rumor mill was awesome to behold.

CHAPTER 21

EVERY STAR HAS AN ANGEL PUSHING IT

While news of the Bentley-Summers phone confrontation over Laura's articles spread through the countryside, Laura continued her writing and speaking out.

Her speeches to the ladies' groups turned into a political campaign. Part of it was the pent-up emotions of women not allowed to vote. This movement that Laura had created was taking on a life of its own.

It was also producing a venom of its own. Bentley was the largest employer in the county. Times were tight, good jobs were hard to come by—and Bentley let everyone know it.

There seemed to be no disputing the mysterious fungus that was blighting the trees. It was the general consensus that if the fungus wasn't stopped they'd lose all the trees in the county. Bentley had the county contract to cut down the acreage around the diseased trees to keep the blight from spreading.

The only debate was over Laura's argument that it did no good to cut some trees to save other trees, if you didn't replant trees. Those against her said there were enough trees in the county and that they'd never miss a few hundred timber acres.

Money ruled in many quarters of the town. Lumberjacks were well paid. The job didn't require a good education, just muscles and guts, and the man who paid their checks got their loyalty. If somebody wanted the trees cut, they'd cut them, no questions asked.

In the Hardacres area, where most of the loggers lived, Laura Ingalls Wilder was not a popular person. One night Michael O'Malley, Bentley's foreman, had a talk with his men.

"Lads, you remember who pays you. Bentley's got the contract and is doing his civic duty to stop this terrible blight from spreading," O'Malley said to the assembled men.

John Flannigan was leaning against the wall. "Seems like that fungus is a godsend. Work's kind of scarce around these parts." As the men murmured agreement he smiled to himself, knowing that he and Jake Carver were the ones really responsible for killing the trees.

"The Lord provideth and the Lord taketh away," O'Malley said, nodding his head.

"O'Malley," said Gene O'Hara, one of the toughest loggers around, "could you shut your trap and pass me the cups?"

A cup of water and a cup of corn liquor were passed. O'Hara took a sip of the water to cool his throat and then a slug of the moonshine. As the liquor seared his throat, he gasped and gulped down the rest of the water.

Catching his breath, he wiped his lips. "Boys, this is good 'shine. Be sure to drink enough water to put out the fire in your throats but not enough to stop the glow in your belly and mind."

"Give me some—pass the cups," said Michael Kelly.

"Hold on, Kelly," said O'Hara. "I just want one more drink."

"Be careful," said O'Malley. "Two drinks will make you want to spit in the pope's eye."

"Watch what you be sayin'," growled O'Hara. "If Father Walsh be hearin' you say that, you've got fifty 'Hail Marys' on Sunday."

O'Hara took his second drink. His face turned red and his eyes started running. Michael Kelly took a long drink without water and fell backward, retching. Flannigan took a quick sip and passed the jug.

O'Malley laughed. "That just shows this is the good stuff."

As the men handed the jug and cups around, they bragged about the way they liked to drink 'shine—some liked it hot, some with brown sugar, some with cloves—but this was pure Ozark moonshine, which would fire up their moods.

The moonshine had the scent of decaying vegetables mixed with any liquid that could make a motor run or a lantern burn. Made in a beat-up copper wash boiler, trickled through old shotgun barrels and pipes, and strained into a galvanized wash tub covered with an old cotton quilt, it was powerful stuff. It ignited the restless fires in the drinkers and fueled their talk of revenge.

Laura Ingalls Wilder was their target, and the more they drank, the bolder they talked. Soon everyone was ready to go do something about it, except for Flannigan, who begged off and slipped away. He had a meeting to attend, he said. What he didn't say was that he had a meeting with his partner Jake Carver to mix the poison to kill more trees.

The other loggers headed toward Apple Hill to vent their frustrations and scare Laura into silence.

There was talk of "wuppin' Manly" and "burnin' the barn." As the men moved down the dusty road lit by the stars, they made plenty of noise.

Eulla Mae Springer heard them coming down the road as they neared the Wilder's and woke Maurice, who sneaked out to take a look and heard them talking about going to Apple Hill. He got out his shotgun and took the back trail to alert his neighbors. Although he had bad memories of night riders, his friends needed his help.

If it hadn't been for Jack the dog barking up a storm and awakening Manly, the loggers gathered behind the barn might have caused some trouble, but Manly, shotgun in hand, quietly rounded the corner of the barn without being seen.

Maurice came up, stood beside him, and whispered, "Want me to fire off a barrel and scare them off?"

"Not yet," Manly whispered.

The men from the Hardacres had decided to burn the barn, but they couldn't find the matches they'd dropped. They were on their hands and knees, patting the ground.

"They be here somewhere—just keep lookin'," said Michael O'Malley.

"Oh, I stuck my hand in a cow pie!" one of them moaned.

"What? Oh, lads, I stuck both my hands in somethin' that stinks!"

Manly lowered his shotgun and just watched the bumbling loggers. He had moved the outhouse the day before and hadn't yet covered the hole, which lay between him and the intoxicated troublemakers.

In the glint of moonlight, he saw the lost matches and picked them up. "Okay, Maurice, fire it off," he whispered.

Maurice's old shotgun let loose with a terrific bang—so loud that the men from the Hardacres who were standing fell to the ground screaming.

"What are you boys doing on my property?" Manly asked, striking a match against his boot and holding it near his face.

"It's him!" O'Malley shouted. "Get him, boys!"

"Be careful where you step," Manly said quietly to Maurice, as the loggers moved toward them. "I moved the outhouse yesterday and didn't fill in the old hole yet."

O'Malley laughed. "Wilder, I'm going to knock the—" He didn't finish his sentence because he'd fallen into the old outhouse hole.

Maurice looked down in the hole and smirked. "O'Malley, you know how to swim?"

"Help, lads! Help! It stinks down here! Get me out!" O'Malley screamed.

It took them a while to pull O'Malley out because each time they got him near the top, someone let go of the rope because he smelled so bad. Finally Manly tied a rope to the fence, and O'Malley pulled himself out.

"Don't come back," Manly said as he and his double-barreled shotgun walked the stumbling drunks to the edge of the property. They were all humiliated—not for what they'd done but because they'd been caught.

When they were gone, Manly walked Maurice to the edge

of his property and stopped to admire the stars. "Maurice, thanks for standin' with me."

Maurice smiled and patted Manly on the back. "Good friends are supposed to do that."

A shooting star passed overhead. "Sometimes I feel that we're like that shooting star . . . moving along all alone in this world."

Maurice rested the shotgun butt on the ground. "Not alone. Every star has an angel pushing it."

Manly looked toward the night sky filled with thousands of stars. "There must be a lot of angels up there, Maurice."

The two good friends shook hands and parted. Maurice called out to Manly in the dark, "You remember you ain't alone. The angels are with you." He looked up at the heavens and chuckled to himself, "And if the angels don't get there in time, why, old Maurice will be by your side."

CHAPTER 22

SAVE THE TREES

Saying Laura was furious with the events of the evening would be an understatement. The next morning Rose was still trying to calm her mother down.

"Mother, sit down. Please, you've got to get a hold on yourself."

"Those men should be in jail. Manly should have marched them to the sheriff's house at gunpoint."

Rose shook her head. "I think Father did the right thing. They were not thinking right."

Laura stamped her foot. "That doesn't excuse criminal behavior."

"But you're not the law, Mother."

Laura walked to the table and folded and refolded a cloth napkin several times. Finally, she turned to Rose and said, "No, I'm not the law. But if the law doesn't step in, then *I'm* going to make sure it doesn't happen again."

"Mother, what are you talking about?" Rose asked with a worried look on her face. "I think you should try to reason with Bentley to calm everything down."

Laura picked up her shawl and headed to the buggy.

"Where are you going, Mother?"

Stopping at the side of the buggy, Laura turned. "I'm going to do what you said. I'm going to reason with Bentley."

Her fury increased when she passed the loggers, who cat-called her from the treetops they were trimming. She parked the buggy in front of Bentley's office and marched determinedly to the door.

Inside, Bentley was looking at the county commissioner, who was wavering on supporting another county culling contract. James Matson said to the men in the room, "This so-called fungus is popping up without a pattern. Is it airborne, or what?"

Bentley shook his head. "What does it matter if it's airborne or is carried by bees? You heard the report of what tree blight has done to other areas of the Ozarks."

Matson shook his head. "I don't know, William. Maybe we should call in an expert from St. Louis or Jeff City to see what's causing this. This thing's striking all kinds of trees, not just one kind, like the blight over in Arkansas."

"Ask your son-in-law, the one I gave a job to," Bentley said pointedly. "He'll tell you how the blighted trees need culling. And besides, this contract will let me hire some of the other young men in town." Bentley looked around the room, catching the eye of each man in the room so they would clearly understand his meaning.

Laura interrupted his pressure tactic by banging open the door. Bentley looked up, clearly embarrassed by her presence. "Mrs. Wilder, you have no right to barge in here. I'm holding a meeting with the county board. Please leave."

Laura looked around at the men she'd known for years

and shook her head. "I suppose this is another county contract being put up for bid with one bidder."

Before anyone could say anything, she walked over to James Matson and patted him on the shoulder. "James, I hear that someone finally hired that son-in-law of yours after he got off the county work farm. What's the name of this civic-spirited company?"

Matson averted his eyes and said, "I think you already know, Laura."

"Just wanted to make sure that our good government was being run as usual," Laura sneered, looking directly at Bentley.

Bentley pointed toward the door. "Mrs. Wilder, this is private property, and I'm asking you nicely to leave."

Laura laughed loudly. "Private property? Bentley, you keep your drunken louts off *our* private property, you hear?"

Bentley laughed. "Now Mrs. Wilder, boys will be boys." Several of the men in the room chuckled along with Bentley, showing their support.

Laura went up to the table and faced Bentley. "If your boys come on our property trying to burn down our barn again, we won't be responsible for what happens."

The men in the room began whispering, so Bentley tried to exert control. "Is that a threat, lady?"

Laura just smiled coldly. "No. Just a statement of fact. Whatever happens will be on your doorstep."

Bentley stood up and pushed his chair back. "Only thing on my doorstep is a welcome mat for everyone but you. Now leave this room! You're disturbing our meeting."

"Is this a county meeting or a den of thieves?" Laura

coldly asked, looking around the room. "Is this the Wright County government or the Bentley Benevolent Society?"

"I asked you to leave. Now I'm going to toss you out!" Bentley said, escorting her out by the arm and locking the door behind her. Turning back to the men at the meeting, Bentley said, "Gentlemen, before we were so rudely interrupted, we were discussing the new signs of fungus that Carver and Flannigan found on the west side."

Carver winked at Flannigan. They both nodded to the men in the room, who were discussing the new signs of fungus blight they'd discovered in the hills.

Bentley stood by Carver. "Jake, why don't you tell these men what happened in Grants Pass, Oregon, when they didn't catch the blight in time?"

Carver stood up. "Certainly, Mr. Bentley." The men then heard about the thousands of acres that were lost because the blight was allowed to spread—how waiting cost the county almost twice the amount it would have cost to cull the trees.

After the meeting, James Matson stopped by to chat with Summers, the newspaper editor.

"Tell me about the county meeting, James. Is Bentley going to get another contract?" Summers asked.

Matson told him about the meeting. He always "leaked" the results of the county meetings to Summers. It had been an unspoken "thank you" for Summers's not running the article on his being arrested during the Blue Masons meeting in St. Louis the year before, when he was put in the pokey for being disorderly.

When Matson finished telling of the report about what happened in Oregon, Summers sat back. "Grants Pass, Oregon, you say? What was the man's name who told about the troubles there?"

"Jake Carver. Said he knew all about it since he was the man in charge of finding the places where the blight was breaking out."

Summers wrote the name down. "Seems I read something 'bout the Oregon blight. Think I'll send a telegraph message out there to find how they stopped the blight."

"That'd make a good story. That's a good idea," Matson replied.

Summers bowed his head. "That's why I'm a newspaper editor. Got a nose for news," he said, tapping the end of his nose.

The next day, Laura organized a group of ladies and took a buggy-line out to see the destruction of the trees for themselves. Kodak cameras were clicking away until Bentley's men came and forced them to leave.

Laura took the buggy-line by way of Bentley's big house and had them all park on the edge of the Bentley lawn. Laura went up and knocked on the door. A young servant answered the door. "Tell Mrs. Bentley that the ladies of town would like to have a word with her."

Sarah came out and, seeing who it was, changed from a smile to a scowl. "Yes? What do *you* want?"

Laura pointed to the women in their buggies. "The ladies of Mansfield want to give your husband a message."

Before she could respond, Laura signaled, and the banner that Manly had painted was unfurled across several of the buggies:

SAVE THE TREES!

It was printed in bold, black letters on two sheets sewn together.

Sarah Bentley looked at the banner. "My husband has gotten your message and thinks you're a foolish woman for not wanting the tree blight stopped properly." Looking Laura in the eye, she said coldly, "What I think of you can't be said in polite company."

She turned to close the door but stopped in her tracks when she saw Laura's dog Jack using her freshly trimmed lawn as a privy. "Get that dog out of here!" she screamed.

Laura started to leave and said over her shoulder, "The message on the banner is for your husband. Since I can't say what I think of you in polite company, the message from my dog is to you."

Sarah stood there red-faced with anger, then slammed the door shut. The ladies in the buggy-line applauded.

When William Bentley heard about the embarrassment his wife had suffered, he went immediately to the bank to put financial pressure on Summers. All he wanted was the bank to call in the equipment note for the new printing press at the *Mansfield Monitor*. The bank took it under consideration, which left the threat hanging in the air for Summers.

Bentley then got some of his friends to cancel their newspaper ads, but Laura countered by contacting the American Forestry Association. She persuaded them to purchase a series of information ads in the *Mansfield Monitor,* much to Summers's relief.

The pleasant little town was siding up along economic lines. The issue of stopping the fungus blight was getting lost in the hostilities. Paychecks were more important than conservation. Rose encountered hostility while eating in town, and Manly was confronted at the feed store by some toughs. No fists flew, but the bolts from angry eyes gave Manly the message.

Laura wasn't to be deterred and wrote another hard-hitting article and delivered it to Summers.

THE FUNGUS IN OUR COUNTY GOVERNMENT
By Laura Ingalls Wilder

Just as we're told that the fungus that is killing the trees in the county spreads in strange ways, I think it is strange that the county government holds its meetings in Bentley's office to discuss the tree culling contracts pending. Why don't they just toss in the towel and turn the keys to the county treasury over to Bentley?

Yes, we all want to stop the fungus, but shouldn't it be done in a responsible way? Shouldn't the contracts include replanting what we cut down? Shouldn't the contracts be let in the light of day and not in smoke-filled rooms?

This would remove the appearance of impropriety and the stench of backroom corruption that is wafting above our ridges.

Just as the fungus is spreading through our trees, so does the fungus of government corruption spread quickly. When a people become accepting of corruption and overlook it because it's "just the way it's done," then in our lifetimes we will see the beginning of the end of America as envisioned by our Founding Fathers. When greed rules, we all lose, and the end is in sight for the greatest experiment in democracy that the world has ever known.

"Laura," Summers said quietly after reading it, "even the title's going to upset Bentley and all our friends in the county government." But he placed her column on the table and began to set the type.

After the article appeared, things turned mean. The window of the newspaper office was broken by a rock with a message attached. "Quit printing her" was all it said. It was more than enough to get the message across.

As the trouble mounted, Laura began to question her aims and motives. Was her thirst for vengeance against Bentley causing unnecessary trouble? People were siding with or against her. Had she put her own feelings above all else?

A person can pretend to hide from the truth, but when you're all alone, you know the truth. Just like cheating at solitaire—you can hide it from others, but you know what really happened and whether it was right or not. And Laura knew, deep in her heart, that her actions had been based more on her own personal anger than on what was right or wrong. When she admitted this to Manly, his only comment was, "You get more by using honey than with a hammer."

The revelation was so clear that she shook her head at her own blindness. "I think you're right, Manly."

"Well, girl, what are you going to do about it?"

Laura rocked back and forth. "I wish I could tell Andrew Summers right now how everything's gotten out of control."

"Well, why don't you tell him?"

Rocking away, she opened her Sears "wish book." Manly knew that her moods could quickly change and saw the slight grin on her face. Laura simply said, "Because I don't have a telephone."

Manly knew he'd been had again as she rocked and smiled.

CHAPTER 23

GRANTS PASS

The telegraph message that Summers sent to the editor of the *Grants Pass Gazette* was overlooked for several days. That wasn't really all that unusual, since newspaper offices are always understaffed and overworked.

Big Bill Triplett, the fatherly editor, publisher, and chief reporter, finally got around to reading the telegram, which had been stuck on a nail over the door:

> To the editor of the *Grants Pass Gazette:*
> I am the editor and publisher of the *Mansfield Monitor* – stop – Terrible problem of tree blight here in Wright County, Missouri – stop – There is no pattern to blight – stop – Seems to affect all varieties of trees – stop – Jake Carver has moved to our town from Grants Pass and told about your outbreaks of blight – stop – Please send clippings relating to blight and how you finally stopped it – stop – Will remit postage if you send a statement – stop – Andrew Jackson Summers.

Big Bill looked at the telegraph message and shook his head. "Hey, Mary," he called to his assistant, "lookee here."

Mary, an older woman whose hands were covered with printer's ink, came in. "Well, I'll be," she said, handing back the message. "Looks like Jake Carver's found himself another place to work that scam. Thought he was in jail."

Big Bill shook his head. "No, there was somethin' 'bout him gettin' out. I think the timber men greased some palms to get him out of the state to keep him quiet."

He walked over to the file drawers and flipped through the back issues. "Aha, here it is!" He held up a fading copy of a newspaper with the blaring headline: "Tree 'Blight' a Fraud —Carver Arrested—Timber Men Connected?"

"Mary, you cut this article out and the others 'bout the blight. Send them along to this editor with the pompous-sounding name."

"Yes, sir, Big Bill," she said.

As she walked away, Big Bill knocked twice on his desk. "And Mary."

"Yes?"

"Send a bill along for postage." He winked. "Fudge a little, will ya?"

CHAPTER 24

SPYING ON SILLY WILLY

"Look at that," Larry Youngun whispered to Terry, "Crab Apple will never beat that race horse."

Terry peeked back over the fallen log. Silly Willy Bentley was racing his sleek, black horse up a short track built for him in the pasture of their farm. Two men held the horse at the beginning of the track and a third waved a flag at the finish line.

"It ain't fair!" Terry moaned. "His pa bought him a fast horse, built a race track, and has men teaching him how to race."

"That's 'cause they're rich," Sherry said.

"Pa says that we're rich in ways we don't even know about," Larry shrugged.

Terry coughed. "I can tell you the ways we're poor that I do know about. We get a penny a week allowance, ain't got a horse, got to wear donated clothes, and our shoes gots holes in 'em," he said, holding up his shoe to show the newspaper sticking through the hole.

"Silly Willy gets a dollar a week allowance I hear," Larry sighed.

"And he gots a horse faster than Mr. Springer's lightning horse," Sherry said, watching Willy race up the track.

"And what do we got?" Terry said, looking down at his feet. "We got Crab Apple, the stubborn mule, who don't even like wearin' a saddle and tosses us into the pig's pen."

"Crab Apple ran fast the other day," Sherry said.

"Only when the hornets were chasin' him," Larry said.

"Maurice said hornets were the key," Terry said, scratching his head.

"I'd hate to open a door lock holdin' a hornet," Sherry whispered.

Willy raced down the track again while the Younguns watched. As he rounded the bend, Larry shook his head. "He's gonna win that ten bucks fur sure."

"Wish he'd fall off or somethin'," Sherry whispered.

Terry scratched his backside and felt his pocket. He'd forgotten about his sling shot. Pulling it out, he winked. "Your wish is my command."

He put a rock into the sling and turned to Sherry. "You promise you won't rat on me?"

"I promise," she whispered, all wide-eyed.

"Are you gonna shoot Willy?" Larry asked.

"Naw, I'm just gonna see if I can hit his horse . . . that's all."

Terry took careful aim. Willy was barreling around the track, acting like he was king of the hill. Aiming high to take in the drop and the distance, Terry pulled back and fired.

The rock shot into the air, arching toward a point in the track ahead of Willy. "I think you shot too far," Larry said, shaking his head.

"Bet you'll miss," Sherry said.

"I'll bet a penny if you'll bet your stupid dolly," Terry said.

"What you gonna do with a dolly?" Sherry asked.

"Gonna drop it down the outhouse," Terry laughed.

"I ain't bettin'," Sherry said.

"Chicken."

"You'll miss anyway," she said, sticking out her tongue.

"Just watch," Terry smiled.

The rock sailed up and down, on a direct path with Willy. "I think you're gonna hit him!" Larry exclaimed.

The rock hit the horse in the rear and sent him off the track. "Help, help!" Willy screamed, trying to hold on.

The horse kicked and reared, tossing Willy around like a rag doll. The handlers and flag man ran over and grabbed at the horse's reins, knowing their jobs were on the line if the crying, spoiled boy got tossed.

Finally, they reined the horse in and walked him to the finish line. Willy wiped his eyes and then sneezed . . . and sneezed and sneezed.

"Look at that?" Willy had to be lifted off his horse at the finish line because he was having a sneezing fit.

"Wonder what caused that?" Sherry asked.

"If we had a Johnson Smith Catalog, I could order some sneezin' powder . . . then we could put it on him before the race and he'd sneeze himself out of the saddle," Terry said.

The ten-cent catalog, filled with novelties, tricks, gadgets, and gag jokes, was the hottest thing for kids to have. Parents hated it because of the unruly behavior it encouraged, but that's what made kids love it even more.

Larry shook his head. "Pa said we weren't ever to send for one to keep."

"I know, I know," Terry shrugged. "He called it a 'compost heap of crude jokes.'"

"Yeah," Sherry added. "Pa said that there were things in there that we shouldn't know about."

"Maybe we shouldn't, but I already do," Terry laughed.

"You do what?" Larry asked.

"I do already know about the things. Saw a copy sittin' in Mr. Pickle's barber shop."

"You better not tell Pa," Larry said. "He'll wup you for lookin' at it."

"It was either that or I read *Police Gazette*."

"Read that and you'd really get a *real* wuppin'!" Larry said. He looked at Terry and said, "Pa says there's somethin' wrong with that catalog."

"Ain't nothin' wrong with it, just has a lot of kid things in it," Terry said.

"Like what?" Sherry asked, very curious.

"If I told you, then I'd be disobeyin' Pa."

"But you already did!" Larry said.

"No," Terry said, shaking his head. "Pa said we weren't ever to send for one to keep. He didn't say nothin' about sittin' in the barber shop and just happenin' to pick up a copy by mistake and lookin' at all the pages before you realized what it was you were readin'."

"I wish I had one to pick up and make a mistake with," Larry shrugged.

Terry didn't want to tell them that he'd already sent for a catalog of their own. Of course he rationalized that he never intended to keep it. He just wanted to borrow it for a long, long time. Like forever.

CHAPTER 25

THE INVITATION

Laura was still thinking about the problem of letting her anger rule her actions as she sat on the front porch the next morning. Talking out loud, she said to a bird that had landed on the rail, "Mr. Bluejay, trying to get to the truth is like walking down a crooked road."

A voice answered back, "That's good, Mrs. Wilder, but sometimes if you go down a crooked road with your eyes closed, you'll be like that gnat that broke his neck goin' aroun' the curve."

Laura was startled and looked at the bluejay. Maurice stuck his head up over the edge of the porch, smiling. "Oh, hi, Maurice. I didn't know anyone was listening."

Maurice wiped his brow. "Eulla Mae said that she heard from Clara the phone operator who heard it from Mr. Chan who was talkin' with Manly that—"

Laura raised her hand to stop him. "What? Who said what to whom?"

Maurice chuckled, "Don't mind the method if the message is right. I heard you were troubled 'bout your quarrel with

Mr. Bentley. Sometimes the answer is right 'round you if you just stop to look."

"I have been troubled," Laura said, closing her eyes for a moment.

Searching for words, Maurice looked up at the sky and then down. "Why don't you and Manly come to our gospel meeting this afternoon and just forget about the tree business for a while?"

"Why, thank you, Maurice. Are you sure we'd be welcome?"

"The African Methodist Episcopals welcome everyone of any color. The only thing is, you ain't welcome if you don't like to eat."

Laura laughed. "Pray tell, what are you all serving?"

Taking a deep breath, Maurice began, "Well, before the service will be a potluck supper of fried chicken, broiled chicken, chicken pie, stewed chicken, chicken wings, some rabbit, possum, butter beans, new potatoes, mashed potatoes, squirrel, pig, cracklins, barbeque, and pigs' ears and tails. Of course there'll be fritters and buttermilk, hoe-cake and sweet milk and cracklin' bread and—"

"Is that all?" she grinned.

"No, ma'am! They also be servin' some bonny-clabber, gooba-peas, fried apples, dewberries, batter-cakes, mushmelons, honeycomb, snappin' turtles, catfish, cider, cornfield peas. That's 'bout all I can think of."

"All? That's quite a feast, Maurice."

Scratching his head again, he added, "Oh, yes, we's also havin' some bacon and greens. Can't forget the greens."

"If everyone ate a plateful, they'd be too sleepy to hear the sermon."

"Not the African Methodist Episcopals!"

"How are the African Methodist Episcopals different from the Methodists?"

"I'll make it simple. If you went into the black section of town with a bunch of newborn kittens and told everyone they were Methodist kittens, they'd be no takers. But if you waited a week and took the same kittens back and said they were African Methodist Episcopal kittens, the whole kitty box would be empty in a flash."

"What difference would a week make, Maurice?"

Chuckling to himself, he grabbed his belt loops and eased back. "Why, the kittens opened their eyes and saw the truth and became African Methodist Episcopals!"

Maurice laughed so hard he had to sit down.

Laura got the message. Was her fight with Bentley like two people sitting on a dynamite keg, both arguing who would be blown higher when the keg blew up?

"Do you want to come?"

"I think I do, Maurice. I think I do."

"Good. It's about time you took some time out to help yourself," Maurice said, smiling.

CHAPTER 26

MAIL-ORDER SECRETS

Meanwhile, the Younguns were busy scheming to win the upcoming horserace. Their father had taken the widow Carla Pobst on a buggy ride to "show her the countryside."

Larry figured out that Pa was looking for a new mother for them, so they tagged behind, sneaking and peeking on their pa. It wasn't long before Pa noticed six eyes bobbing up and down behind trees and rocks and heard their giggles. He gave them a piercing glare which sent them all scurrying home.

On the way back to their house, they came upon the mailman on horseback. "Got anything for us, Mr. Long?" Terry asked.

Mr. Long was a kindly mailman, part-time volunteer fireman, and sometime dogcatcher, and he liked the Younguns. No matter what they did or what kind of trouble they got into, they had a sort of "aw, shucks" attitude that melted anger away.

"Well, kids, I've got two letters for your pa, and I think there's something here for you, Terry."

Larry and Sherry looked at Terry, who smiled. "Must be my Johnson Smith Big Book."

"You sent for it?" Larry asked. "Pa said you couldn't have it."

"Yup, here it is," said Mr. Long, interrupting them. "Here's a catalog marked 'Terry Youngun.' "

Before Mr. Long was twenty horse paces away, Larry was all over his brother.

"Pa said you couldn't have that catalog. Said it had bad things in it."

Terry opened the catalog and smiled. "Brother, I'm not going to keep it. I'm only borrowing it from the Johnson Smith company. I intend to send it back."

"You do?" asked Larry.

"Yes . . . with an order for something we need for the big race."

Terry walked along, laughing to himself. Sherry peeked inside the book and broke out laughing at the pictures. Try as he might, Larry just couldn't help but sneaking a look at the Johnson Smith catalog that Sherry and Terry were engrossed in.

From the ten-cent catalog you could buy novelties, live animals, lizards, scientific supplies, jokes, hobby supplies, planes, boats, magic tricks, gadgets, cameras, optical goods, books, guns, jewelry, disguises, costumes—the list went on and on.

"Look at this!" laughed Terry, "You won't believe it!" Terry held up the advertisement.

ANARCHIST STINK BOMBS
The Rankest of Rank Jokes.
More Fun Than with a Limburger Cheese.

Consists of small blown-glass vials, containing in liquid
form a chemical which will produce a most horrible odor.
One dropped in a room full of people will cause more
consternation than a limburger cheese.
People will say while holding their noses: "Woo Pu," "Say
boys, someone has a limburger here," "My, oh my, what
smells so bad?"

ANARCHIST BOMBS
1 BOX OF 3 VIALS FOR ONLY 10 CENTS!

"Anarchist Stink Bombs! Pa's not going to like this!"
Larry exclaimed. Then he thought for a moment. "Say,
what's an anarchist?"

"Ah, you know," said Terry, who didn't really know. "Pa
said they are troublemakers and toss bombs."

"Do anar-ar-ar—" Sherry stumbled on the word.

"Anarchists," said Terry.

"Yea, do these whatever-they-are toss stink bombs at people?" she asked.

"Look, Miss Million Questions," Terry said, lifting the
book above her head, "this book is for kids—big kids like
me. These things are supposed to be funny. Johnson Smith's
Big Book ain't something you're goin' to bring to Sunday
school."

"Yea, and you can't tell Pa that Terry has it." Larry said.
"He called it a 'compost heap of crude jokes.' "

"Look at this!" Terry squealed. "This is too much!"

SNEEZING POWDER!

Place a very small amount of this powder on the back of your
hand and blow it into the air and everyone in the room or motor-

car will begin to sneeze without knowing the reason why. It is most amusing to hear their remarks, as they never suspect the real source but think they have caught it one from the other. Between the laughing and the sneezing, you yourself will be having the time of your life!

Only 10 cents!

So much for their Sunday school lectures! For the rest of the way home the three of them fought over who would hold the Johnson Smith catalog.

Let their elders have the old Sears "wish book." The Johnson Smith Big Book was filled with itching power, sneezing power, exploding matches, and whoopee cushions.

This was a catalog that offered tools of mayhem for children with great imaginations. It described a thousand ways for weaklings to get even with bullies, for the righteous to avenge wrongs in a humorous way. Every page was exciting and offered something to scream about.

"Hey! I need this ventrillo in school!" Terry screamed.

"A what?" asked Larry.

"A ventrillo. Here, look at the ad," Terry said, pointing to the opened page in the book.

THROW YOUR VOICE

Into a trunk, under the bed, under a table, back of the door, into a desk at school, or anywhere. You get lots of fun fooling the teacher, policemen, peddlers, and surprise and fool all your friends besides.

THE VENTRILLO

is a little mouth instrument that fits in the mouth out of sight. You can imitate all kinds of birds, animals, etc.

Only 10 cents!

"What would you do with it?" asked Larry.

"Why, I could make you sound like a frog and make people think Sherry was a goat."

"Can not, can not," Sherry screamed, hitting her brother.

"Ribbet, ribbet, baa-baa," Terry croaked, racing ahead with the catalog in his hand.

Terry Youngun was convinced that inside this catalog was their secret edge to win the upcoming race. "We'll have to spend some money to make money" was his rationale for whatever he was going to order. They caught up with their brother around the bend. He was sitting on a log, chuckling to himself.

"Let's get this!" Sherry squealed.

Larry looked at the ad she was pointing to. The people were holding their noses and looking embarrassed. "A 'whoopee cushion'?" he asked.

"Read the ad to me, Terry, please!"

"All right:

WHOOPEE CUSHION!

The Whoopee Cushion or Poo-Poo Cushion as it is sometimes called, is made of rubber. It is inflated in much the same matter as an ordinary rubber balloon and then placed on a chair. When

the victim unsuspectingly sits upon the cushion, it gives forth noises that can be better imagined than described.

Only 15 cents!

Sherry stopped in the middle of the road.

"What kind of noises?"

"You know."

"No. What happens when you sit down on it?"

"It makes a whoopee noise," answered Larry.

"What's a 'whoopee noise'? Like a party horn?"

Terry slapped his hand to his forehead in exasperation. "No, dummy, like gas! Flatulence."

"Fla-two-what?" Sherry asked.

"Poo-poo wind, silly."

Sherry smiled and then scratched her head, perplexed again. "How do they get that inside?"

"Oh, Sherry," Terry groaned, snatching the catalog from her hands.

As they walked down the road, Sherry kept up the questions. "How do they get it in there, huh? How many are in there? Can you put 'em back in once they slip out, huh?"

Larry said to Terry, "You've opened up Pandora's box with that one."

"Yeah, Terry said, trying not to listen to his sister's questions. "Pandora's poo-poo wind box."

Terry rolled his eyes as his sister's questions continued all the way home.

CHAPTER 27

THE AFRICAN METHODIST EPISCOPAL CHURCH

Dr. George greeted Laura and Manly at the door of the African Methodist Episcopal Church. "What a surprise! I didn't expect to see you folks here today. Did you come to speak about trees?"

Laura was at a loss for words.

The good doctor couldn't help laughing at Laura's discomfort. "I'm just jokin' with you, Laura."

Laura smiled. "I know you are, doctor. We just came to enjoy the meeting."

"You missed all the food. Want me to have the ladies get you both a plate?" Dr. George asked, pointing to the ladies cleaning up under the canopy of trees.

Laura looked at Manly, who shook his head. Laura said, "No, thank you anyway. We just ate."

Inside, the choir was warming up, and the congregation murmured like an audience about to see a show as they began to file in.

"Come on in, both you. Hurry!" whispered Eulla Mae.

As Laura and Manly entered, Dr. George said, "Laura, Old Man Bentley has been mighty sick. I wonder if you'd come with me to talk and minister to him after the service."

Laura thought to herself, could this be the honey to solve their differences?

She looked at Dr. George and quietly said, "I'd be honored." Then they turned and walked into the church together.

The choir began a fast-paced gospel hymn, and the whole congregation began clapping along. Manly and Laura sat next to Eulla Mae and Maurice. Dr. George sat beside them in the aisle seat.

The church wasn't as fancy as the one in town, but it was filled and moving in unison. As the choir sang its heart out, Laura and Manly couldn't help moving and clapping along.

From behind the choir came "Travlin' Revren' Jones" who went from hollow to town to camp meeting, "preaching the word and exciting the crowds."

Dressed in red satin robes with his hair slicked back, he sent shivers of energy to everyone in the church.

Holding up his hands, he hollered out, "Brothers and sisters, I have come to bring you the Word!"

"Amen," answered the congregation. "Amen, brother."

He led everyone in a string of gospel songs and went among them blessing the young and old ones. They had all lived on the hard edge of life, with few material goods, but there was no doubting their faith in the face of their troubles. Both Laura and Manly truly enjoyed the service.

After the service, Manly gave Maurice and Eulla Mae a ride home and promised to meet Laura at Old Man Bentley's just

as soon as he could. Laura accompanied Dr. George to Bentley's place, about a mile down the road.

Pulling into his driveway, they both immediately noticed the general state of disarray. The weeds hadn't been pulled, the garden hadn't been hoed or cleaned, and there were only a few pieces of kindling on the back porch next to the kitchen.

They found Old Man Bentley on the porch, looking sickly, with a knit blanket over his legs and a shawl around his shoulders. Dr. George had said he was "sick inside" and if he didn't want to get better, he would just wither up and die.

Laura had seen the same look on other people too tired to go on.

"Hello, Laura," Old Man Bentley wheezed. "I hope you're still givin' that son of mine the dickens."

Laura laughed. "Some say I've been doing that, but I've been wondering what I've really accomplished, except divide the town."

While Dr. George began examining him, Old Man Bentley said to Laura, "If the founding fathers of our country had waited for everyone to agree, we'd still be bein' taxed to death by the Brits."

"That's right," Dr. George said, looking under the old man's shirt.

Old Man Bentley coughed, then caught his breath. "Sometimes you've got to get off the fence and take a stand. I like your columns—you need to keep writin' 'em."

Laura reached out and touched his hand. "Thanks, but I've been told by your son that he doesn't like what he's reading."

Dr. George had Old Man Bentley cough, and then Bentley

continued. "Readin' and understandin' are two different things. You could say it in five different languages, but if it's not his way, he won't listen."

They talked a while about farming and the harvest coming and about getting prepared for winter. Laura led him down this path of conversation because there wasn't any chopped wood by the house.

Dr. George took the lead. "Mr. Bentley, why don't you have any wood chopped up for cookin' and heatin'? You're sittin' out here all wrapped up when a good fire would keep you warm."

Old Man Bentley shook his head. "My rheumatism hurts too bad to swing the axe."

"Why doesn't your son—" Laura caught herself in mid-sentence.

Old Man Bentley shook his head. "My son? He doesn't have the time! He's too busy makin' money and buyin' things for that wife of his. He's too busy to help his old father."

By the time Manly came to give her a lift home, Laura and Dr. George had talked with the elderly man about faith and folks who help those in need. Somewhere along the way, Laura came up with a honey of an idea.

REVENGE

While the information from Grants Pass about the fungus fraud made its way slowly through the U.S. mail, the whole town was awash with posters and banners for the Independence Day celebration and race.

Jake Carver had found a completely new outbreak of fungus to the south of town, and even Summers was advocating emergency measures to stop the spread of the blight. A citizens' petition circulated, demanding that experts be brought in to analyze the tree disease, which seemed to spread without rhyme or reason.

Laura took the opportunity to try to lower the tension and preach for reconciliation. Her articles caught the town off balance, since no one expected them. The Wilder-Bentley feud was still the talk of the town.

Needless to say, editor Summers was pleased and quite relieved. Bentley had forced some of the paper's advertisers to pull their ads, and the bank was putting pressure on him about the outstanding loan. Though he stood by Laura, Summers hadn't been sure how long he could hold out financially.

Even Bentley didn't know what to think about the new

tone in Laura's column. He thought it was some sort of trick and looked for hidden meaning in her words and phrases. There was nothing devious. The articles reflected the direction and understanding that she had decided upon. Maybe reason could do what anger couldn't.

A PLEA FOR UNDERSTANDING

By Laura Ingalls Wilder

Perhaps it is time that we sat down and reasoned together. Preserving our woodlands and stopping the fungus is important —can't everyone at least agree on that? There has to be a reasonable middle ground between protecting the local jobs and ensuring that there will be trees to harvest and admire long after we are gone.

Just as the woodlands provide safe haven and breeding grounds for wildlife and game, so do they provide jobs for the timber industry. Without proper conservation efforts to replant what we cut down, there will be no habitat for wildlife or jobs for humans in this area in the future.

Yes, we will stop the fungus, but at what price? Will Wright County look like the barren prairies that cover half this country? Will it be a sea of stumps and weeds when we are old and gray?

Though it will be hard to protect the woodlands and not hurt the economy, it will never get easier unless we start now. If we will all stop the shouting and begin to listen, perhaps we will plant the seedling of the idea that future generations will be proud of.

Understanding, not anger, is the best course of all.

As he read her latest column, Bentley dropped his feet from the desk and looked at it again. "What's this woman up to?" he said to himself.

"What is Laura Ingalls Wilder up to?" was the question in almost everyone's mind. Laura was keeping her own counsel. She wasn't speaking out or leading any more buggy-lines to the lumber areas. She was staying at Apple Hill Farm, tending to her family.

What she had set loose in the town could not be turned off so easily. Laura hadn't changed her opinion, just her tactics. By not letting anyone in on her secret, she left her friends and admirers confused. Bentley thought he had cowed Summers and Laura.

Meanwhile, Flannigan and Carver had taken it upon themselves to look around the ridges and wooded areas bordering Apple Hill Farm for signs of the blight. It wasn't a coincidence that they soon found what they were looking for— right in the same place they'd drilled the trees a week before.

To make Bentley's day, Jake Carver and John Flannigan marched into his office. "Don't know if this is good news or bad news," Carver said, unrolling a land map.

"What you got there, Jake?" Bentley asked, putting the newspaper down.

Flannigan laughed. "Found the blight in a new place. Right near your friend's farm."

"Friend's farm? Who's the unlucky person?" Bentley asked with concern on his face.

Carver slowly chuckled. "Blight's breakin' out all 'round Apple Hill Farm."

Bentley looked at the map and smiled. "This couldn't have happened to a nicer . . . woman." The three men laughed, and Bentley pulled out a bottle of good scotch. He filled three shot glasses. "To Apple Hill Farm," he toasted. "May the blight be stopped on her doorstep!"

Carver toasted and laughed. "Your wish could be our command." Flannigan laughed, too, but Bentley didn't catch their inside joke.

Bentley immediately called for an emergency county council meeting and offered a discount on the next two culling contracts, if one of them was the land around Laura's farm.

He gloated over this turn of events and began circulating an unnamed "expert's opinion"—Jake Carver's—that an experimental method would be to clear all the woods in a certain area and on the farms around it. Perhaps the blight was being spread by some of the local farmers themselves.

Summers himself rode out to tell Laura the news. "Looks like the county's goin' to issue the contracts to Bentley right away."

"Why are they rushing so fast?" Laura asked. "Can't they wait for the experts to get here from St. Louis?"

"You know how it is with an election year comin' up," Summers said, shaking his head.

"Dadgum politicians!" Manly said. "I'd like to take a shotgun to town and talk some sense into Bentley and his political cronies."

Summers put his hand on Manly's shoulder. "Talk like that won't do you any good."

"But what can we do?" Laura asked. "I don't want the woods around here stripped to the ground."

Summers paced the room. "I sent a telegraph message to the editor of the Grants Pass, Oregon, newspaper, asking for information."

"Oregon?" Manly exclaimed. "Why Oregon?"

"They had a similar problem out there. Bentley's main

expert on the fungus, guy named Jake Carver, was out there when they had the outbreak."

"How'd they stop it?" Laura asked.

"That's what I wrote him 'bout. I want to see how they caught whatever was causing it."

After Summers left, Laura was in a worse quandary than before. Events were coming around like a burning circle to engulf her beloved Apple Hill Farm. What should she do? Bentley had thrown down her olive branch of peace and was declaring war, offering to attack the woods around Apple Hill Farm at a cut rate.

There was something about this fungus that just didn't seem right. She'd never heard of a tree blight that attacked any and every tree. If the woods around their home were to be saved, she needed to stop the loggers and find out more about the disease. The only way she knew how to fight back was with words.

Laura left the house to walk and think. After crossing the creek, she climbed up the rock ledge. Standing on the same large boulder she had stood on when she'd first surveyed the land over a decade ago, she remembered how much work the land had needed then. It would take a miracle to save it this time.

Her memories were interrupted by the sound of axes chopping trees and an echoing laugh. On the far side of the ridge Bentley was standing on a boulder staring back at her, mocking her through the gloating smile on his face.

Manly tried to get the county to hold back on the contract to stop the blight around Apple Hill Farm, but the commissioners wouldn't listen. Laura suggested trying to buy the contract from Bentley, so Manly swallowed his pride and went to Bentley's office.

"I'll give you ten percent of the contract's value, right here and now, if you'll sell it to me," Manly said coldly.

"Sell it to you?" Bentley laughed. "You're no logger! With that crippled leg of yours, you couldn't even climb the ridges, let alone climb a tree with spikes."

"I want the contract, Bentley. What's your price?" Manly said, looking him square in the eye.

Bentley just laughed at him. "Why don't you just sell me all your land and move back to the prairie?"

Manly bristled with anger. "I'd never sell you Apple Hill Farm."

"Why not?" Bentley laughed. "You'd make a nice profit! And I'd turn your house into a juke joint for my workers. It'd be a nice, quiet place for them to hang around. 'Course, you'd have to cover up the outhouse hole I heard about."

Manly limped out in anger, Bentley's laughter echoing in his mind all the way home to Apple Hill Farm. He found Laura sitting on the ridge, watching the loggers cutting down the beautiful trees.

"You don't have to tell me. I knew he wouldn't sell you the contract."

"No. He's dead set on takin' his revenge on you through the woods around the farm. He offered to buy Apple Hill Farm and turn it into a juke joint with liquor and women."

How could she stop this man? Why had her initial efforts to save the woods down the road come back to haunt her?

Her thoughts were shattered by a crashing sound. Across the ridge, another of the tall, beautiful trees had fallen. Laura bowed her head.

"Lord, I wanted to save the trees you created. I wanted to protect the land you made and our beautiful orchards. If I took actions that you disapprove of, punish me, but don't punish the land. Don't let Bentley strip the land around Apple Hill Farm or take our land. I don't want to lose another home."

CHAPTER 29

POISONED FRUIT

Early the next morning Jake Carver and John Flannigan walked through the orchards of Apple Hill Farm. Carver winked and said, "Ain't no problem puttin' the fungus to these trees."

"How many you think we need to do to scare 'em off?" Flannigan asked.

Carver thought for a moment. "Wouldn't take long to kill a couple hundred of 'em."

Flannigan whistled, looking at the orchard. "Seems a shame to kill these good fruit-bearin' trees."

"Trees can grow again, but paychecks, why, once they're gone, they're gone for good."

Carver set to work poisoning apple trees with no rhyme or reason. He wanted to make it look like there was a fungus growing and that the trees would have to be cut down to save the orchard. *If it could be saved,* he chuckled to himself.

"You know," he said to Flannigan while he drilled into

another tree, "in Oregon, we did the same thing to a man's groves who was also a troublemaker."

"What happened?"

"Well, I just killed enough trees to make the man think that he'd lose them all. Then we sent a man lookin' like a tenderfoot buyer to town, lookin' for orchards to buy. The man who'd been causin' us problems, claiming we were lyin' about the fungus, went and sold his place, lock, stock, and barrel."

"Did he tell the buyer about the fungus?" Flannigan laughed.

"No, greed got the better of him . . . he took his money and his conscience and ran. When he found out later that the buyer was a ringer for the big boss man, well, he knew he'd been had but there wasn't a durn thing he could do about it."

The sky darkened and Flannigan shook his head. "Looks like it's gonna rain. What say we pack up and get on back before we get drenched."

Carver poured the poison into the hole in the majestic apple tree and stood up. "We'll come back soon and do a few more."

"Let's wait until after Independence Day . . . we've been workin' too hard and maybe we're pushin' our luck."

Carver slapped the poison bucket. "Don't need luck, when you got this stuff."

"When are we goin' to tell Bentley . . . and ask for our raise?"

"If we do the job on Apple Hill Farm right, I think the time is just about here."

"Yeah," nodded Flannigan, "we need to get paid for the fruits of our labor."

"You mean the poisoned fruits, don't you?" Carver smiled. The laughter of the two men echoed across the ravines around Apple Hill Farm.

CHAPTER 30

BENTLEY'S QUESTION

Bentley was a tough man on the outside. He'd been that way all his life.

His father had been a tough man who'd developed a drinking problem after his wife had died. Bentley could remember his father slurring his words, trying to teach his children right from wrong.

With the farm going downhill and the children looking ragged, his father finally quit drinking. He had lost almost everything. Bentley would never forget how his father had gathered the children around, told them they were broke and that he'd let the family down. Then he said his drinking days were over and begged their forgiveness.

These were tough words for a young man to hear from a father he'd idolized, but a lesson that had remained with him all his life—accepting responsibility for what you do.

After his mother died, Bentley grew apart from his father. As his business grew and his father became less able to get around, Bentley looked on his father's needs as something he could pay others to attend to. It was just a matter of business.

So instead of going round to visit his father on a weekly basis, he had his hired hands go by and check on him. They were supposed to see to his father's needs—like chopping wood and weeding his garden—but hired hands had no stake in the job, and Bentley's father was too proud to complain.

All this was going through Bentley's mind as he rode his horse through the Wright County countryside. It was the only way he could be alone, without his wife, son, or a group of fawning employees following after him, wanting something.

After riding through the back roads, he doubled back around the north side of town. He remembered how as a young boy he'd ridden these same roads on the family plow horse as his father walked beside him, father and son together, each trying to learn from the other.

A sudden urge to visit his father struck him, and he took the ridge cut across from Apple Hill Farm to get to his father's house. The sky was darkening, so he wanted to get there before it rained.

As he came over a small rise, he almost ran over Jake Carver and John Flannigan, who looked surprised to see him. Flannigan was carrying a bucket, and Carver had a drill and a long metal veterinarian's syringe in his hand.

Bentley reared back his horse. "What are you two men doing out here? Thought you were working on the south contract today."

Carver grinned. "We've been checking for outbreaks of the blight."

"Thought you'd already found a small outbreak up here," Bentley said.

Flannigan laughed. "We did, but we thought if we looked hard enough we might find some more. Might even find some on the Wilder woman's property."

Bentley felt something wasn't right. "What's in the bucket, Flannigan? And what are you using the drill and horse thumper for?" he asked, pointing to the syringe.

Carver shook his head. "I've got my own methods for finding the fungus. You have to check inside the tree base to find it sometimes."

"Yeah, you have to look all over," said Flannigan, looking up as the first raindrops hit.

A sudden downpour engulfed them, and Bentley shouted as he rode off, "You boys come 'round soon and talk to me about these methods of yours."

"Okay, boss," said Carver.

Bentley rode down the ridge, jumping the gully and skirting a thick briar patch. As lightning cracked across the sky, he decided to visit his father another day.

While Bentley rode out of sight, the two men grinned at each other. "That was a close call," said Flannigan. "Think he knows what we've been up to?"

"That man only thinks of one thing—money. He'll probably thank us, once we tell him," Carver said.

"Still think that's a risky thing," Flannigan said, shaking his head.

"If he don't like it, we'll just take our fungus business to another state. Plenty of men out there don't mind makin' money the easy way."

"What if he turned us in?" Flannigan asked. For the first time he felt concern over what they'd been up to.

"I'd kill him before he could do that," Carver said coldly.

Flannigan looked at Carver and, for the first time, saw the evil glint in his eye.

CHAPTER 31

INDEPENDENCE DAY

The arrival of Independence Day was a welcome relief for the town. Everyone seemed in unspoken agreement to call a temporary truce to the tree war.

The streets were lined with red-white-and-blue bunting. Old Glory hung from the flagpoles and rooftops. Children lining the streets carried flags and were dressed in their Sunday finest.

Dogs had been taken off the streets, and the smell of corn dodgers, cotton candy, and roasting sides of beef filled the air. Children had gotten up early to shoot off firecrackers and guns, to beat drums and blow whistles.

It was a time of patriotism, cooked beef, cakes, and pies. The grand parade of "Ancients and Horribles"—a prairie holdover—was going through town, with the local merchants and officials jumping around in masks.

It was as if the ghosts and goblins of Halloween appeared at a summer party with the scary masks and outrageous costumes. It was a time for the high and mighty to dance along with the hired hands and day laborers.

To strangers, this was a curious tradition, but for Wright

County, it was like having their own version of Mardi Gras combined with all the festivities of the Fourth of July.

Handbills about the parade had been plastered all over the town:

DON'T MISS THE ANCIENT AND HORRIBLE PARADE!
THE DISORDERLY ORDER OF EVENTS

At 3 P.M. sharp, the procession of ancients and horribles, consisting of all classes, sexes, and conditions of people and things, public and private, military and pacific, will be drafted and forced into line in the following order:

First the ancients of the town:
Rev. Youngun with the old lady in the shoe
Sheriff Sven on foot, disguised as a midget
Dr. George in the costume of a burglar
Lafayette Bedal imitating an honest man
Chan of China dressed like a cowboy
Charlie Camorata the piano teacher leading
a 3½ piece band sandwiched between
barber Billy Pickle as a dill, and
Father Walsh as a Methodist, along with
Rose Wilder in the costume of a Gibson girl, and
Thomas Campbell as a cheapskate,
followed by
Stephen Scales, the king of the telegraph pole, carrying the
Grand Old Flag and dressed as a flagpole with
"Four Eyes" Johnson saluting it.

The highlight of the parade was Mr. Chan bumping into Four-Eyes Johnson, who tripped into Sheriff Peterson, who stepped on the Rev. Youngun's old-lady costume. It was like a line of dominoes with arms and legs flapping around. To make matters worse, a couple of the local roustabouts tipped over a horse trough next to the pile-up of bodies, and they all ended up covered with mud!

After the parade, the local school band stood in the town square playing "Yankee Doodle" to a group of mothers leading their children in song:

> Yankee Doodle went to town,
> Riding on a pony,
> He stuck a feather in his hat,
> And called it macaroni!

The problem was that a group of wisecrackers were singing "Good Old Mountain Dew" from the front steps of Tippy's Saloon:

> There's an old hollow tree down the road there from me,
> Where I lay down a dollar or two.
> I go round the bend, and when I come back again,
> There's a jug full of good old mountain dew.
>
> Well, the preacher rode by with his head held high,
> Said his wife had been down with the flu,
> And he thought I ought just to sell him a quart
> Of that good old mountain dew.

With about twenty loudmouths singing the chorus, enough was enough—especially the part about the preacher looking for moonshine. Rev. Leonard Moses from the Congregational Church went up to one of his wayward church members, who had closed his eyes, wailing out the chorus:

"Oh, they call it good ol' mountain dewww . . . "

He only stopped singing when he realized the others had stopped singing and looked down with embarrassment.

"Oh, er . . . hi, Reverend. I was just . . ."

Rev. Moses hit him with his hat. "You weren't 'just' 'cause you already done it. I smell whiskey on your breath, and I heard you makin' fun of preachers."

"But, but—"

"But nothin'! You get on outta here now!"

Rev. Moses looked at the assembled drunks and said, "You men should be ashamed of yourselves for taking up the devil's ways!"

Vendors were selling soft drinks and candy. Firecrackers popped in the air, courtesy of Mr. Chan, who had imported them all the way from China. On the platform set up the day before in front of the hotel, local Congressman Hawkins was reading the Declaration of Independence to all within hearing range.

A band of aging Confederate soldiers marched out in ragged but clean gray uniforms, proudly carrying the stars and bars. A cheer broke out from some in the crowd, and the band good-naturedly broke into "Dixie," which interrupted the congressman's speech.

Laura came to town to try to forget about the trees for a day. She and Manly watched the parades and events. There was a greased-pig-catching contest for the kids, a sack race, and a watermelon-seed-spitting contest. The volunteer firemen of Mansfield challenged the next county's firemen to a fire-tank pull. The older boys joined with their fathers in the log-splitting contest and the greased-pole climb.

Everything was good-natured fun. People laughed during the hog-calling contest and were amazed when Lafayette Bedal won the "drive a nail" shoot. It had traditionally been a "shoot off the turkey's head" contest, but when the good people of the town decided that wasn't teaching good lessons to the children, they switched to nails.

One of the big events of the day was the log-rolling contest, which the Hardacres loggers always won. Everyone competed, even the farmers, but the Hardacres men were used to walking on logs.

Lafayette Bedal was the first to be dunked, followed by Dr. George and piano teacher Charlie Camorata, who sang in Italian to try to throw his Irish opponent off balance. The crowd got the biggest kick when Sheriff Sven Peterson was dunked by the man he had arrested the week before for disorderly conduct. As farmer after farmer got dunked to the laughter of the crowd, it was announced that this year "Mr. William Bentley himself" was entering the contest.

You drew your opponent from a name in the hat and prepared to get wet. Luck of the draw, they said. Everyone had let disagreements fall by the wayside for the day—except Bentley. There was no end to the revenge he wanted to extract for the humiliation he felt he'd suffered from Laura's articles.

Around the small pond everyone gathered to see who would be joining him on the log. Flannigan slipped the judge a five-dollar bill and had him fold the piece of paper with Manly's name on it. Flannigan wanted Bentley to have a turkey on the log—Manly.

When Manly's name was drawn, a lot of people suspected that a ringer had been thrown. The Hardacres men were catcalling and laughing for Manly to come forward.

Jake Carver slapped Bentley on the back. "We're all bettin' on you, boss."

"Bettin'? Is there any question about who's goin' to get knocked off the log?" Bentley laughed.

"No, sir! We're bettin' on how many seconds it will take!" Carver replied.

Bentley suddenly remembered the bucket and tools Carver and Flannigan had been carrying up on the hill by the Wilder's. "I thought I told you and Flannigan to come by the office and discuss what you were doing up on the north ridge."

Carver winked. "We'll be talkin' to you soon. You can count on that."

On the other side of the log pond, Laura looked at her husband. "Manly, you don't have to do this."

Manly smiled bravely, under the circumstances. "I don't have a choice. I've got to live in this town."

Lafayette Bedal came up. "Manly, want me to take your place?"

Manly shook Bedal's hand. "No, a man's got to do what a man's got to do."

"But your leg, Manly. He knows what the stroke did to you," Laura pleaded.

"Can't change that, can we now?" Manly said, winking at her as he walked to the edge of the contest pond.

Manly and Bentley squared off on each side of the log. Hardacres men steadied the log as they listened to the judge's countdown. Manly had taken off his shirt and boots, but Bentley had kept even his coat and tie on.

"You're lookin' mighty confident today, Bentley," Manly said, nodding a greeting.

"You'd be confident, too, if you were log rollin' with a cripple," Bentley said. The Hardacres men snorted with laughter.

The judge called out, "Ready . . . set . . . let 'em loose, boys."

Manly tried to control the log, but Bentley was a master. Bentley moved the log back and forth, playing with Manly the way a cat plays with a mouse.

"I'm surprised you didn't have your wife take your place," Bentley sneered.

Trying to keep his balance, Manly retorted, "Sticks and stones, Mr. Bentley. Sticks and stones."

Moving the log back and forth, playing with Manly and delaying the inevitable, Bentley said, "Sticks and stones will be all that's left surrounding that property of yours! That fungus is a curse on your wife's big mouth!"

Manly's bad leg began to buckle under him, but he caught himself before he fell into the water.

Bentley saw Laura standing on the side, watching with worry, and he shouted out, "Hey, Mrs. Wilder! You were worried about trees falling. Well, watch your husband—Timmmberrr!"

He dropped Manly into the pond and then purposely rolled the log over on top of him. Manly came up gasping for air, smacking his head. For a moment he was dazed, unsure of where he was.

As he reached out his hand for one of the Hardacres men

in the water to help him, the man withdrew. Manly fell back into the water, bumping his head on the log again. The people from the Hardacres—Bentley's people—laughed mean-spiritedly.

Maurice Springer helped Manly from the water, and Laura and Eulla Mae took him to sit under a shade tree while they cleaned the cut on his head. Anger filled Laura as she thought of the cruelty inflicted on her husband. Maybe honey was not the way to change this wasp called Bentley after all. Maybe it was time to fight back.

Summers came up. "How's Manly doin'?"

"I thought he'd need a stitch or two, but Eulla Mae fixed him up." Laura turned back toward Bentley and his men. "Look at them over there, gloating like bullies."

"See that man standin' beside Bentley?" Summers asked Maurice.

Maurice looked over. "I've seen him 'round, but I don't know him."

"Name's Jake Carver. Told the county all 'bout what happened when the fungus blight hit Grants Pass, Oregon," Summers said.

"What's he do for Bentley?" Laura asked.

"Claims to know how to spot outbreaks of the blight," Summers said. "So far, he's been right on the button, knowing where to look every time. He and that no-good John Flannigan."

Maurice looked again. "I saw them couple of weeks ago, lookin' 'round the wood areas across from Apple Hill and down yonder by the creek bend—carryin' a bucket and a tool of some kind."

"Probably just takin' samples of the blight they found,"

Summers said, kneeling down by Manly. "I got some information on what happened in Oregon comin' by mail. Should be here any day now."

Manly stood by Laura and looked at Carver and Flannigan. "Those two sure do look like trouble."

"Hey, Summers!" Lafayette Bedal shouted from across the edge of the log pond. "When are you going to pick up your mail from Oregon that was delivered to me by mistake?"

"I'll get to it tomorrow. This is a holiday," Summers shouted back.

"I'll bring it to you tonight at the dance. I'm tired of waitin' for you to come and get it. And I'm tired of waitin' for you to pay your bill," Lafayette laughed.

"Oregon?" Laura exclaimed. "Isn't that the information you've been waiting for?"

"Probably," Summers said.

"You know anyone else in Oregon?" Laura asked.

"Probably not," he said. "I just didn't want to think about it until after the holiday. This is the first happy day the town's had in a long while."

CHAPTER 32

IMPERIAL WATER HORSE

On the other side of town, the three Younguns and Dangit were walking down the street as innocent as little angels. But they had a certain look in their eyes that their father immediately recognized. Dangit hid behind the nearest building.

"Larry, Terry, Sherry, what have you been up to?"

"Nothin', Pa," they all said in unison.

Rev. Youngun looked at Sherry. "Is that the truth, girl?" Sherry didn't answer. "You come with me," he said and walked her around behind the nearest building.

"Don't rat," Terry whispered to her as she inched by him.

Out of earshot of the two boys, Rev. Youngun got down on one knee and eyeballed her carefully. "Sherry, I want you to tell me what your brothers have been up to."

Sherry shook her head. "Can't, Pa."

"Why?"

She whimpered, " 'Cause I said I wouldn't say anything—they made me swear."

"Hmm," he said, rubbing his chin, perplexed. "All right, I'll just ask you three questions, and you shake your head for no and nod your head up and down like this for yes. Understand? Okay?"

Sherry nodded yes.

"Did you do anything that you should tell me about?"

Shake, shake, shake.

"Good. I didn't think so. Did Larry do anything that you should tell me about?"

Shake, shake, shake.

"That sort of surprises me."

Terry and Larry peeked around the corner. Terry whispered to Larry, "She's rattin' without rattin'."

Rev. Youngun continued. "Did your brother Terry do anything that you should tell me about?"

Sherry sat there as still as a statue. Out of the corner of her eye she caught the glare of Terry's eyes. He was pounding his fist in his hand, nodding his head up and down. It was the "I'll get you" sign.

Sherry was so nervous watching Terry nod up and down while pounding his fist that she fell into the same rhythm and began nodding her head up and down. Her father took that as the answer to his question.

"I thought so! Now let's go talk to your brother."

"We better get back out front. Pa would know somethin's up for sure if he sees us peekin'," Larry whispered.

Rev. Youngun and little Sherry came marching around the corner. "Boys, I'm going to ask you again. What have you both been up to?"

Larry looked hurt. "Up to, Pa? Why we've just been walking the racecourse to get to know it for the big race."

"Are you sure that's all?"

"We did something with one of the race markers, Pa," Terry whispered.

Their father smiled. "Isn't it better to tell the truth?"

"Yes, Pa, but . . ."

"But what, son?"

"Well," said Terry, kicking a dirt chunk off his boot, "we did put back up one of the marker signs that had fallen."

"That was a good deed son, a good deed." Tousling Terry's hair, he added, "Now you children run along and have some fun."

It was fun they intended to have! Of course Terry didn't tell their father that yes, they had put the sign back up, but now it wasn't pointing in the same direction. It just happened to point through the graveyard—and that wasn't all they'd planned!

The big race was announced. Bentley had built his own reviewing stand across from the judges. He came up talking loudly and issuing commands to the unlucky employees who didn't duck out of his way in time.

Sarah Bentley sat under her pink umbrella, drinking lemonade and showing off her jewelry. William Bentley, Jr., sat by her side, resplendent in his red and white silk racing suit with matching hat. One of his father's hired hands was holding the reins of his expensive horse next to the stand.

Within earshot of Sarah, Lafayette Bedal said to Sheriff Peterson, "That boy Silly Willy looks like a big fat candy cane!" The Sheriff guffawed, but when he saw the bolts of anger coming from Sarah's eyes, he quickly tipped his hat and went off to check the town.

The Younguns had talked Maurice into holding Crab Apple behind the feed store until the last minute, but the mule was kind of impatient. Every time Maurice turned around, the mule nipped him. Dangit just sat there watching.

"Ouch! Dangit! Now stop that, you stupid mule! Who ever heard of a mule entering a horse race, anyway?" Dangit the dog ran over and nipped Maurice on the leg for using his name like that. "You crazy dog!" Maurice shouted, jumping up and down on one foot.

Crab Apple pointed his mouth up and "hee-hawed" several times. Dr. George came around the corner and looked at Crab Apple. He'd never seen a mule with a bandana holding his ears back flat and white stripes painted on his sides.

"What's that, Maurice, a 'zee-mule'?" Dr. George asked.

"Zee-mule?" Maurice questioned, looking around.

Dr. George laughed. "Yeah, with those stripes it looks like a cross between a zebra and a mule."

Maurice shook his head in disgust. "Huh! No, this is Crab Apple. Those crazy Youngun kids painted him up and talked me into keepin' him hushed back here till they're ready to race."

"Well, you're not doin' a very good job about it. You can hear that mule on the other side of town."

Larry Youngun had walked back around to get Crab Apple. "Hey, Maurice, the race's about to begin."

"Who's goin' to race this thing, you?" Dr. George asked.

Larry patted Crab Apple. "No, Terry is. We're going to watch."

Handing the reins to Larry, Maurice guffawed. "You watch? I'll bet you kids got somethin' up your sleeve!"

Most everyone in the county was gathered on the street to watch the big kids' race. All the entrants had been told to follow the pointed arrows around the outskirts of town. The first one back would win a ten-dollar bill.

Silly Willy strutted out with a kiss from his mother and pat on the back from his father. "Yuck!" said Terry. "That kid makes me sick!"

"Come on, get on," said Maurice. "Say, I thought you said Larry and Sherry were goin' to help you get goin' in the race?"

"They will, Maurice. They will," Terry said with a sly grin.

The judge announced, "Children, mount your horses," to the delight of the crowd.

Ten country boys rode forward on a motley assortment of plow and buggy horses. Only Silly Willy had a horse bred for racing. When Crab Apple was brought forward by Terry, Silly Willy behaved like a chip off the old block. "You call that thing a horse? That's a mule!" Silly Willy laughed.

Terry just looked ahead and said, "This is a rare imperial water horse. The kind that races for the emperor of China."

Silly Willy looked at the mule with the bandana holding his ears down. The bandana was so tight that it pulled Crab Apple's eyes back.

While this was going on, the other two Younguns were putting out part of the arsenal they'd spent their life savings on. As Terry had said, they had to spend money to make money.

Sherry was walking in front of the starting line and dropping Spit Devils everywhere, except near where Crab Apple would start. She was following the directions in the Johnson Smith Big Book, which read: "Just place them on the ground and when stepped on the result is one continuous succession of loud reports, just like a repeating pistol or a whole pack of firecrackers going off at once. Price: 10 cents per dozen."

Larry had taken a lit cigarette he'd found near the saloon and stuck it in the fuse of the Day-Go Bomb, carefully following the directions: "Place the Bomb firmly on the ground —light fuse, retire to a safe distance, and watch the result. The contents of the bomb are shot away up, exploding in the air with a terrific bang."

Larry placed it at the first turn around the block.

When the judge said, "On your mark," Terry tossed three Anarchist Stink Bombs in front of Silly Willy. As the smell drifted across the street, people began holding their noses. "What's that awful smell?" one of the boys asked.

"I passed gas!" People thought Willy had said it, but it was Terry using the Ventrillo, which was a ten-cent device he'd sent for to "throw your voice." Everyone thought that Silly Willy had said it because Terry had mastered the devious art of throwing his voice.

The judge held his nose and said to the men on the podium, "What's that kid been eating?" The men around him laughed uproariously until the judge quieted them and started again. "On your mark . . . get set . . ."

Sherry released the Sneezing Powder, and within seconds everyone from the judge to the riders was sneezing. Even the horses were snorting. Since Terry had cotton stuck up his nose, he wasn't affected.

"Ah choo! On your . . . ah choo! . . . mark, get set . . . ah choo!"

On the word *Go!* Larry sprinkled the Itching Powder down from the rooftop, and as the horses took off, stepping on the Spit Devils, they began rearing up. Most of the riders couldn't hold on, because they were sneezing and itching at the same time that their horses were going loco over the war-zone rat-tat-tat of the Spit Devils.

There was general pandemonium in the crowd. Sarah was itching, William Bentley was sneezing, and it smelled so bad that most people were holding their noses when they weren't sneezing.

Crab Apple took off at a fast trot and got a good lead on the rest of them. Larry and Sherry took the shortcut to the change in the course they'd planned.

Silly Willy was the first to get his horse under control and come racing after. He rounded the first corner just as the Day-Go Bomb exploded. His horse reared up and bucked him off.

After a few minutes, the race was on again. Silly Willy raced forward, with the plow horses plodding along behind.

At the bend Terry passed the sign that had been changed to point into the graveyard. Larry took off to hide behind the graves, and Sherry stood by the sign to point the way to the other riders.

Silly Willy came along first, and Sherry screamed out the message she'd give to them all: "Hold your breath in the graveyard, or you're the next to die!"

Well, Willy and the rest of them got into the graveyard, and the race slowed to a crawl. There were sticks and branches blocking the way so they couldn't race. The farther in they got, the redder their faces got from trying to hold their breath.

It was spooky, and they were running out of breath. The Younguns had bought a goblin mask and tied it onto Dangit the dog, who came barking out from behind a gravestone. One of the plow horses reared up.

Larry came out with a pirate mask on, and the riders who got control of their horses rode every which way, screaming as they went. Silly Willy got control of his horse and took off toward town. He knew the Younguns were behind it all!

Meanwhile, Terry was rounding the last bend, thinking that the last half-mile was his to race alone. But Crab Apple had a mind of his own and was tired of racing. He just stopped, meandered over to the nearest tree, and began scratching himself.

"Come on, Crab Apple! Don't fail me now!" Terry pleaded.

"Hee-haw, hee-haw," answered Crab Apple.

Terry saw the finish line ahead and turned and saw Silly Willy coming as fast as lightning down the hill.

"*Please,* Crab Apple. I'll be nice to you every day."

Crab Apple responded by turning around and nipping him. What was Terry to do? They'd spent their $3.86 life savings on the Johnson Smith arsenal, and if he didn't win, they'd be broke!

There was a buzzing overhead. Terry looked up. Crab Apple looked up. A hornet's nest! Should he take a few stings and win the race?

Silly Willy passed him by, giving them the nose tickle sign in defiance!

Terry stood up on Crab Apple's back and snapped off the branch that held the big oval nest. Hornets flew around, and Crab Apple began moving in circles.

With the nest held just behind his rear, Crab Apple took off like a blaze of glory. He was running so fast that Terry could hardly hold on. Hornets were everywhere, and they were catching up with Silly Willy.

As Terry and Willy neared the finish line, they were neck and neck. But when a hornet stung Silly Willy on the nose, he fell back, and Crab Apple crossed the finish line first. The hornets scattered the crowd.

Maurice laughed uproariously. "I knew hornets was the key! I knew it!"

Rev. Youngun was pretty sure Terry's victory was less than legal, *or* Christian. So as the judge was announcing the winner and handing Terry the ten-dollar bill, Rev. Youngun stepped up on the platform. Terry almost had the bill in his hand.

"Thank you, judge," said Rev. Youngun. "My son Terry told me that if he won the race, he'd donate the money to the church mission society to bring the Word to the heathens."

Terry squawked, "I did n—" He stopped when his father's foot pushed down hard on his own.

The judge looked at Terry with pride. "This boy is a credit to his family, a credit to the community." He patted Terry on the head.

Terry looked as if he was about to be sick as the judge said, "Everyone come to the big dance tonight and watch the fireworks."

Rev. Youngun gathered his three children behind the stand and looked them sternly in the eyes.

"I know that you three did somethin' to win the race. Maybe it was those firecrackers or whatever, but you did somethin'."

"Pa!" exclaimed Sherry.

Rev. Youngun put his hand over Sherry's mouth. "Hush! I know you did somethin' as sure that I know that the sun's goin' to rise tomorrow mornin'."

Their father began rubbing his hands together, flexing his fingers. A wuppin' was on the way!

"What you goin' to do to us, Pa?" Sherry whined.

Rev. Youngun thought for a moment. "Since Terry gave the prize money for the Lord's work and nobody seems to have gotten hurt, I think that I will . . ." They were hanging on his every word. ". . . yes, I think that I will just let you all go have a good time today. Here," he said, reaching into his pants pocket, "here's a nickel for each of you. Go have a good time."

A nickel! Each of them had thought that a wuppin' was coming, and now they had nickels in their hands.

Rev. Youngun stood there smiling. "Well, what do you say?"

"Thanks," said Terry.

"Thanks a lot, Pa," said Larry.

He looked at Sherry. "Well?"

"I prayed you wouldn't wup us, and the Lord gave me this—" she said, opening her palm, "—a miracle nickel."

Rev. Youngun just laughed.

CHAPTER 33

PARADISE LOST?

"Cod in heaven, what are we gonna do now?" Manly asked, looking at the dying limbs on the apple tree. "This fungus is gonna wipe us out."

Laura took the branch from his hand and fingered the curling leaves. The whole tree seemed to be drawing into itself, as if it was sick to its stomach.

Manly looked around and counted out loud. "One, two, three . . ." he paused. "There must be ten trees scattered in here that have got to go."

"I hate losing them," Laura said. "Isn't there anything we can do?"

"We don't want to take the chance and lose a thousand other trees. Only way to stop a blight is to cut out the bad ones. It's better to replant a few trees than have to start again."

Laura closed her eyes. *Start again?* It seemed like that was the story of her life. When they came to Missouri, it was to plant roots and bring some stability to their lives.

If the fungus spreads to the other trees, she thought, *it will destroy Apple Hill Farm. Then the place wouldn't be worth a tenth of what it is now.*

Would we be able to sell it? Where would we go? The old wagon is still in the barn, but there aren't any more pioneers. There's just motor cars, trains, and a civilized world out there now.

Laura looked around her beautiful farm. *This is my paradise . . . my paradise found . . . and now it might be paradise lost. It's not fair! It's not fair.*

Manly saw the tears rimming Laura's eyes and put his arm around her. "You remember leavin' the Dakotas in that old wagon and landing here with barely nothin'?"

Laura nodded and smiled, drifting off into thought. Back to August, 1894, twelve years ago.

They'd come to Missouri, to start again. To find their promised land and make a last stand of salvaging their lives. It seemed like yesterday—not twelve years ago—when Manly had brought their wagon to a halt at the edge of this rugged farm land.

It was not what she had expected. Covered with sassafras, sharp thickets, steep slopes, heavy woods, and rock strewn ridges, Laura's first impression had been one of disappointment.

"The salesman said there's a pond nearby," Manly nodded.

"What else did he say?" Laura asked hesitantly.

Manly looked around. "Said there's all kind of wonderful things we got here. Good soil, fresh spring water, lots of game and . . . and over there's the orchard the man told me about," Manly said, pointing proudly to lines of apple trees, left to rot.

"*A bit of an exaggeration,*" *Laura mumbled to herself.*

"*Look at them apple trees,*" *Manly winked, trying to get her excited about the place.* "*The salesman said there were over 800 of 'em. Why, with a little tending, we can make this into a fine, fine orchard.*"

Laura looked at the nursery row of trees set out in the worn out fields. She shook her head. "*They look half-dead.*"

"*But they're still half-alive,*" *Manly smiled.*

Laura knelt down and fingered the soil. "*The land's worn out. It's so poor that you couldn't raise corn over four feet high.*"

She looked around. Most of the trees had still not been planted. "*Manly, who'd buy apple trees if they haven't even cleared the land for them?*"

"*That's why the deal's so good,*" *Manly smiled.* "*The man who owned the place didn't know what he was doin'.*"

"*We're just a couple of prairie tenderfoot dirt farmers. What do we know about growing apples?*" *she asked.*

Manly bent a branch with a small apple on it. "*Enough to know that if you tend these trees, clear out the brush and fertilize 'em proper, we can grow the finest apples in all of Missouri.*"

She took the branch from his fingers and let it go. Just needs water and tending, she thought to herself.

Laura came back to the present. The branch in her hand was not one filled with promise, but of disease, death, and despair. She walked among the trees, touching the healthy ones and stopping at the dying ones.

They had come to Missouri with just one hundred dollars to their name. This was about all they could afford, and after twelve years of hard work, they had built something, really built something for themselves.

And now it was being threatened by this strange disease.

"It's not fair," she cried out to Manly.

"I know it's not, girl, but we can't undo what the good Lord's done."

"He wouldn't do this to us," she said. "I've already had enough taken in my life."

She thought about losing the prairie house to the Indians, Pa selling her favorite cow, losing her son, losing their house to the fire in the Dakotas. *Why . . . why?* she asked herself.

"Some things just can't be explained rationally," Manly whispered, smoothing her hair. "It ain't the end of the world . . . if we have to, we can always start again." He spun her around and danced a jig to cheer her up.

"Why, we can move to the city . . . you always wanted to be a city girl. I'll be a butcher, Rose will be a baker, and you can be a candlestick maker."

Laura smiled and then began laughing. Manly grabbed her arm and they danced a jig together in the dust, then spun around until they clung together. As they hugged the world away, Laura knew that they could face anything as long as they were together.

We were just a couple of tenderfoots when we bought this place, Laura thought, *but Manly and I pulled it off.* She looked at the sick trees and knew what had to be done.

"Let's cut them down," Laura said. "Cut them down, burn the branches and pull up the roots. It's the only way."

"We'll replant what we cut down," Manly said. "There's no way we're gonna lose a single tree on Apple Hill Farm."

CHAPTER 34

NEW PARTNERS

"Do you like my dress?" Sarah asked her husband.

"It looks fine, just fine," he mumbled, not paying her much attention.

"Do you think all the women will notice?" she said spinning around. "But then, they always do. I wonder what that Laura Wilder is going to wear?"

"Maybe she won't come," Bentley said, his mind elsewhere.

"Well, I bet she won't be wearing a dress like mine. It's direct from New York," she beamed, spinning around in front of the mirror. "And it only cost two hundred dollars."

That caught William Bentley's attention. "Two hundred dollars! Why, my mother never spent more than two dollars on a store-bought dress in her whole life!"

"Oh, William," she laughed, twirling for herself, "Your mother wasn't married to a rich man like I am!" She danced over and kissed him. "And she wasn't married to such a handsome man as I am."

She took him by the hand and danced around the room. "I'm going to be the belle of the ball, aren't I, William?"

"That's why I married you," he smiled.

She moved her head back and forth, humming a dance tune. "Do you think we can go visit New York soon? I so miss the parties and the dances. Let's go in the fall, want to?"

Bentley, who had long ago gotten over trying to be someone he wasn't, shrugged. "I don't know, Sarah. Lumber business is going strong . . . I don't think I could take the time off now . . . maybe you should go without me and visit your folks."

"Money, money, money. We've already got more than I could spend on Park Avenue in a lifetime," she laughed. "What you need is to spend time back home with the real people. We could go to the opera or to a society dance and . . ."

"We're goin' to a dance tonight," he whispered, nuzzling her ear.

"Dance? This is more like a barn dance," she said snidely. "But in the Ozarks, beggars can't be choosers. I just hope they don't play "Turkey in the Straw" all night long again."

Bentley sighed and hugged her. *I guess I have spoiled her,* he thought. *I wanted a society girl from New York and that's what I got . . . only here she's a duck out of water.*

"Does your shoulder still hurt?" she asked, noticing him wince when she hugged him.

"Must have pulled a muscle on the log roll, that's all."

"I'm so glad you dumped that Manly know-it-all Wilder into the pond. I just wish it would have been that hateful wife of his instead. I'm still mad at her harassing me in front of the ladies of the town."

"She does need some coolin' off, don't she?" he laughed.

"And those minister's kids! You know they cheated Willy out of the prize money. Who ever heard of a mule beating a horse in a race?"

The servant came up and knocked lightly on their bedroom door. "Mr. Bentley, there's two men to see you downstairs."

"Who are they?"

"A Mr. Carver and a Mr. Flannigan. Said they had something they needed to tell you."

"William, tell them to come back tomorrow," Sarah frowned.

"This will just take a moment," he said, leaving the room.

Carver and Flannigan were waiting at the front door. Carver spoke up, "Mr. Bentley, we just wanted to drop by and tell you that we think that blight's goin' to keep spreadin' onto Apple Hill Farm."

"You might just get that place at a bargain price if the blight keeps spreading," Flannigan laughed.

"What do you mean, you think it's goin' to keep spreadin'? How can you predict it?" Bentley asked.

"Just something you get to know," Carver shrugged. "I learned all about how this fungus works during my two years figurin' it out in Oregon," he winked.

"Well," Bentley said, "this blight might be bad for some, but it's certainly been good for business. Now boys, if you'll excuse me, I've got to get ready for the dance."

Flannigan cleared his throat. "Ah, Mr. Bentley, what we came to talk to you about is gettin' a raise from all the business we're doin' and . . ."

Bentley held up his hand. "You came to my house on

Independence Day to talk about a raise? Can't this wait until tomorrow at the office?"

"Just seems like we need to be compensated for all the work we're bringing you," Flannigan said.

Bentley paused, wondering if he was hearing him right. "Work you're bringing me? I know you boys are good fungus spotters, but it seems like the work is comin' from a blight in nature."

"Not everythin's as it seems in this life," Carver said coldly.

"And just what does that mean?" Bentley asked.

"Exactly what you think it means," Carver said, eyeing him.

"And just what kind of raise do you boys have in mind?" Bentley asked, knowing that something was not right about this whole talk.

"Oh, we were thinkin' 'bout goin' into business with you," Carver smiled.

"I don't need any partners," Bentley said.

"I think you already got some," Flannigan winked. "And I think you know more than you're lettin' on."

"Yeah . . . partner," Carver said, slapping him on the back.

Somethin's goin' on here, Bentley said to himself. *Somethin's not right.*

He remembered seeing them with their bucket and drill near Apple Hill; how they always seemed to know where to look for fungus outbreaks, how it didn't start until Carver got here and . . . and it all seemed too coincidental. But he didn't know quite what to make of it.

"We'll be by in the morning to talk about our new deal,"

Carver said. "Come on, Flannigan, let's go celebrate our new venture." The two men walked off into the darkness, laughing loudly.

Sarah called down from the bedroom, "Come on, William, we're going to be late for the dance. Get your suit on."

Bentley walked back up the stairs, deep in thought. *Now I'm waiting for the other shoe to drop. I'm into something so deep that I can't see the forest from the trees.*

CHAPTER 35

DANCIN' FIREWORKS

By nightfall the Independence Day celebration was in full swing. Children were setting off fireworks behind the buildings and under the wagons.

Someone had stuck a "Kick Me" sign on the back of Sheriff Peterson, but no one had dared to do it yet. If they'd stuck it on Silly Willy's back, the line of takers would have gone around the block.

Most of the adults were hovering in and around the big striped tent where a small band was tuning up for the dance. Laura had always loved dancing and could remember her grandmother letting loose with a fast jig in the kitchen.

Manly couldn't dance because of his limp, but he'd never stopped Laura from dancing with their friends. After she'd agreed to marry a farmer, he couldn't deny her the pleasure of just-for-fun dancing if his leg wasn't up to it.

Dr. George came up and stood beside Laura. "We'll be by, organizin' a help-out for Old Man Bentley tomorrow. Can we count on you both?"

"Oh, Doc, let's talk about it tomorrow. Tonight's for dancing!" she exclaimed to the world, throwing her arms up.

"Okay, okay," he said, turning away. "I'll come by tomorrow." His words were drowned out as the caller announced a new set. "Choose your partners, ladies. Couples to your places."

The music began, and the couples of Mansfield reeled around the floor. Sven Peterson was swinging his wife around, and Rose was already on the dance floor with a young man named Travis Reaux, who had moved to town from Texas. Manly was trying to keep a special eye on Rose and the young man because she had that "young girl's fancy" look in her eyes as she spun around on the dance floor with the handsome Westerner.

The Hardacres couples gathered off to the side, laughing at one of Father Walsh's jokes.

"Sashay back!" shouted the caller. Laura began tapping her feet.

"Sixteen hands held up high," went the call. Laura was moving around in a half-circle. Watching her wiggle, Manly smiled.

"Swing your partner round and round and bring her back to me!" Sheriff Peterson bumped into Stephen Scale, the telegraph operator. They both laughed.

"Four hands up," shouted the caller, dancing around.

Song after song went by. The "Virginia Reel" was followed by "Bile Dem Cabbage Down," the "Acadian Waltz," the "Soldier's Joy," and the rakish song that no one requested but everyone seemed to dance to, "Where'd You Get Yo' Whiskey."

Dressed to the nines, the Bentleys stepped onto the dance floor and reeled around, showing off.

"Hope he slips," whispered Manly.

When "Bow-Legged Rabbit" was announced, Laura sang along:

> Bow-leg-ged rabbit, A box ankle Joe,
> Flea bite me so bad I can' dance no mo',
> Don't dance me down boys, don't dance me down.

Then the caller cried out, "We're going to do the 'Hillbilly Reel!' " and the dance floor was packed. The tent was hot and steamy. The faces of small children could be seen peeking under the flaps, hoping to see their parents dancing.

"Would you mind if I danced with your wife, Manly?" Lafayette Bedal asked.

Laura looked to Manly with hope in her eyes.

"Laura, you want to dance with this Frenchman?" Manly asked mischievously.

Nodding her head and grabbing Lafayette's hand, she was out on the dance floor in one step. While Lafayette and Laura spun around, Manly stood at the edge of the floor, clapping along.

"Did you give Summers his letter from Oregon?" Laura asked as Bedal spun her across the floor.

"It must have not been what he wanted. I gave it to him a few moments ago. He sure looked upset at what he was reading."

It was obvious that the crowd was delighted with Laura's dancing, which infuriated Sarah Bentley. As the couples spun around the dance floor, Sarah maneuvered her way around and "accidentally" bumped into Laura and Lafayette, knocking them off balance.

The Bentleys spun away laughing, so Laura did a cross-the-center cut and rammed directly into them. Laura and Bedal spun away laughing this time, while Sarah stood and glared.

The caller sang a rhyme to cool the tempers. "Ladies, ladies, let's be ladies, now all grab hands and stop actin' like babies."

Lafayette grabbed Laura's hand as the caller brought the music to a halt. "Ladies, pretty ladies, listen up now," he said, wiping the sweat from his brow. "We're going to have a little schottische-jig dance contest for the ladies only. Now everyone circle 'round."

As the younger girls entered the circle to compete, Laura walked back over to Manly.

"Why aren't you entering that contest, Laura?" Manly asked, kissing her on the cheek. "Your ma and grandma were the best jiggers around."

Before Laura could answer, she saw Sarah Bentley step inside the circle. "That woman thinks she's the belle of the ball," Laura muttered.

"What did you say?" asked Manly.

"Oh, nothing, Manly. I think I *will* enter the contest."

Summers came, pushing through the crowd, waving a newspaper article. "Laura. Laura, you've got to read this."

"Not now, Andrew," she said, turning him away. "I've got some dancin' to do."

"But . . . but . . . ," Summers stammered.

"No ifs, ands, or buts, Andrew," Manly laughed. "Her feet are jumpin'!"

As Laura walked away, Summers turned to Manly. "Then you read this!" Summers said, shoving the article in his face. "I think the whole fungus business is a fraud."

Laura stepped inside the dance circle as the music started. It was a fast, red-hot jig. You had to keep up with the music and not miss a beat, or the caller pointed you out of the circle.

Laura kept up with the younger girls, moving her feet as fast as she could. She was pushing her body, but if Grandma could dance the jig when she was seventy, so could Laura!

From twenty ladies it was soon down to fifteen, then ten, then five. Sarah Bentley had survived the cuts, dancing surprisingly well for such a stuck-up woman, Laura thought.

Laura danced over toward her and asked, half out of breath, "Did you dance the jig at your society parties in New York?"

Sarah laughed, "We had to learn this in our primitive history class at finishing school."

Laura was gigged by this horrid woman, who was not even the least bit winded! Her anger gave her a second burst of energy. There were now only three ladies left—Sarah, Laura, and one of the Hardacres girls, who was getting all the Irish cheers.

"Dance for the green, girl. Dance for the green!" laughed Father Walsh.

Sarah danced a circle around Laura and laughed in her face. The Hardacres girl tried some fancy footwork, but a misstep sent the auburn-haired beauty back to the Hardacres crowd for consolation. Now it was down to two—Sarah and Laura.

The competition was as intense as the pace. The caller kept up a nonstop patter and pushed the band to play faster and faster. Laura thought her heart was going to give out.

Feet up, feet down, in what seemed like a blurred motion

of a hundred steps a minute—Sarah still didn't appear winded, but Laura was almost down for the count.

From the corner of her eye Laura caught a nod or sign between Sarah and her husband, who was on the edge of the dance ring. William Bentley was giving his wife the "push her" sign.

If Laura hadn't seen it, their plan would have worked. Instead it spurred her on to a final effort.

As the two closed in tighter, Laura maneuvered the dance over toward the food and punch bowl table. Sarah followed closely behind her, looking for that "innocent" opportunity to push her over.

Laura ducked as a "slipped elbow" swung by her head and bent backward as a hip came her direction.

Trying to time it just right, Laura spun around and bumped her hip sideways at just the exact moment that Sarah was bending backwards. Sarah was caught off balance and went tumbling on top of the table, landing with her rear end in the punch bowl.

You'd have thought that everyone's funny bone had been tickled at the same time. Sarah was sitting there like a wet hen, and before her husband could pull her from the punch bowl, Manly had clicked a picture with Laura's box camera!

As another square dance was called, Laura and Manly sneaked away from the laughing crowd. Outside, Bentley was holding his sobbing wife.

"I've never been so humiliated," she moaned.

Bentley saw Manly and Laura and stepped in front of them.

"Move aside, Bentley. We've no fight with you," Manly said.

"What's wrong, crip? Let your wife do all your fightin'?" Bentley said.

"I may have a crippled leg, but at least I ain't a fraud," Manly said.

"What are you talkin' about? Who are you callin' a fraud?" Bentley demanded.

Laura could feel Manly tense up and begin to make a fist. "Don't, Manly. Don't fight him."

Manly stepped forward. "It's been coming down to him and me for a while. Might as well be now."

Bentley laughed. "That's right, Mrs. Wilder. It's time your man stood up like a man."

Bentley began rolling up his sleeves and stepped forward with fists in the air. Manly limped a step, circling slowly.

"Stop! Stop!" shouted Rev. Youngun, pushing them apart. "In the name of God, what's gotten into you two?"

"It's none of your business, Reverend, so move out of the way." Bentley shoved the minister and clipped Manly on the jaw with a left uppercut.

Manly stood his ground and rubbed his jaw. Instead of hitting back, he came to his senses and helped Rev. Youngun back to his feet.

While Manly was dusting off the minister's coat, Bentley took a hard, fast swing, but not fast enough. Rev. Youngun caught it with his hand and spun Bentley's wrist behind his back.

"I said no fightin', you hear?"

Hiding wide-eyed on the side were the Younguns. They'd never seen their father take action against anyone!

Terry whispered to Larry and Sherry, "He's better than the Durango Kid any day."

"Let me go, Reverend. Let go before you get hurt," Bentley growled.

Laura saw her cue. "First you try to hit a man with a limp when he's not looking and push a man of the cloth. Next thing you'll tell me is that you fight old men like your father."

Rev. Youngun relaxed his grip and released Bentley. Laura stepped forward until she was eye to eye, toe to toe with Bentley. Though the night sky exploded with fireworks of all colors, it could not match the anger spewing out from their locked gazes. Some of the Hardacres men started to come outside the tent, but Father Walsh pulled them back in.

"I forced you to stop writing about my business. Everything in newspapers is a pack of lies," Bentley sneered into her face.

Before Laura could answer, Summers's voice broke the venom in the air. "Lies? How 'bout the fungus fraud in Grants Pass, Oregon, that your man Jake Carver was arrested for? You call that a lie?" Summers asked, walking forward with a newspaper in front of him.

"What are you talkin' about, Summers?" Bentley asked. He was taken aback over the headline of fraud and Jake Carver's picture on the front.

"Seems the timber men were workin' a county contract scam in Oregon, culling trees over a mysterious blight," Summers said smugly.

Bentley looked at the article. "I have no idea what you're talkin' about, Summers."

Laura took the newspaper article and scanned it. She read out loud, ". . . and Jake Carver's method of spreading the so-called blight was to poison trees at random by drilling

The *Herald*

**FUNGUS BLIGHT
FOUND TO BE
FRAUD!** TREES
POISONED

holes into their bases and injecting poison. In the trial, the prosecutor called it a 'bucket of blight' that Carver carried around, killing hundreds of trees."

Bentley was speechless. He clearly remembered Carver and Flannigan with the bucket, drill, and syringe. Carver had found all the blight outbreaks—claimed to have a sixth sense about where to look.

The moment of truth hit Laura and Bentley at almost exactly the same moment. Bentley took his wife by the arm. "You go on home. I've got to find Carver and Flannigan."

"And the sheriff," Manly added.

"Were you in on it, Bentley?" Summers asked.

Bentley turned to Summers and then looked directly at Laura. "No. I like to work hard and make money, but I'd never do something like this. You've got to believe me."

Laura said quietly, "You don't have to convince me— you've got to convince them." Bentley looked at the silent crowd circled around and sighed deeply.

CHAPTER 36

GOOD NEIGHBORS

The next morning, Dr. George and Rev. Youngun brought a group of friends and neighbors to the Wilder's. They had their tools in their wagons, along with their wives, kids, assorted dogs, and baskets of food.

"Doc, what are you up to this morning?" Laura asked.

"I told you last night that we need to do a help-out for Old Man Bentley. These folks are comin' out as good neighbors to get his place back into shape."

Rev. Youngun said from his wagon, "Have you seen to-day's paper?"

"No," Laura said. "We're still kind of in shock over that Oregon information."

"Well, hold on to your boots," exclaimed Rev. Youngun, "and take a look at this." He unfolded the morning newspaper. It was a special banner edition, with the headline in bold ink.

FUNGUS IS A FRAUD!
TWO TREE KILLERS ARRESTED!
BENTLEY CLAIMS INNOCENCE!

Laura took the paper and read it while Rev. Youngun talked. "Sheriff said that Wright County's not the only place Carver did his dirty deeds."

"What about Flannigan?" Manly asked. "He's from 'round here, ain't he?"

Dr. George spoke up. "Seems that Carver promised him a share if they could talk Bentley into going along with their scheme."

"I might not like Bentley," Laura said, "but I can't see him participating in this kind of fraud."

"Summers says he was duped like the rest of us," Doctor George said.

" 'Cept he got paid good to be a dupe," Manly said quietly.

"Time's a-wasting. Are you comin' with us to Old Man Bentley's?"

Before Laura could answer, Manly got his hat and tools and headed to the barn to hitch up the wagon. It looked like a twenty-mule team as the wagons pulled into Old Man Bentley's place.

He was sitting in the same spot she'd last seen him, huddled under a blanket on the front porch. They all climbed down from the wagons, greeted the elderly man, and just started to work. He'd helped older folks when he was a younger man and knew what these neighbors were up to. It's hard for a proud man to say much more than thanks, but what goes around comes around. It was his turn for help now.

As the men cleared the weeds from the garden, cut the grass, trimmed the trees, and chopped wood, some of the women cleaned his kitchen and house while others prepared baskets of food for everyone to eat.

Old Man Bentley was overcome with emotion at the good neighbors he had. His rheumatism was bad, and with the arthritis locking his joints, they all understood that he had to sit on the porch and watch them do all the work.

With crosscut saws and axes, they took possession of his woodlot. At noon a wood saw was brought in, and it sawed briskly all the afternoon. By evening there was enough wood ready to last a year!

Sarah and William Bentley stopped their buggy at the edge of the entranceway, Silly Willy riding his horse behind them. Bentley had come to visit his father because he needed to talk. He needed the advice of the one man he knew who had come back from a harder situation than Bentley was in now.

When Bentley saw what these folks were doing to help his father out, he had to stop before pulling in. He stared a long time at the scene in his father's yard.

With a deep sense of shame over the events of the fungus fraud and over strangers having to help his own father, Bentley drove slowly up the drive. Silly Willy rode behind them, staring at the people. A silence came over the happy, working crowd as the Bentleys drove up next to the porch.

Bentley looked at his father. "What are these people doing?"

Old Man Bentley just sat there with the blanket wrapped around him, staring ahead as if his son weren't there.

"Can you hear me, Pa?"

Old Man Bentley shook his head. "I heard ya! These folks are helpin' an old man, doin' what a son should be doin'."

Bentley turned slowly and looked into the faces of the

people of Mansfield, faces he'd taken for granted, thinking everyone had a price.

The kitchen door banged open, and Laura came out to hit a rug against the front rail. "Why's it so quiet out here?" she said happily. When she saw William Bentley, her mood darkened. "Oh, it's you."

Manly walked up to the side of the porch carrying a load of kindling and looked at Bentley. "Are you here to pick another fight?"

Bentley's face turned red as he stammered, "I . . . I . . . I'm sorry. I'm sorry for the way I've treated you, Manly. I'm sorry for what I said."

Laura cleared her throat. "Sorry won't help the woods around town or Apple Hill Farm."

Old Man Bentley spoke up. "You stupid fool! Why are you wastin' your time hurtin' and beatin' 'round the bush? You need to apologize to these people."

Bentley climbed the porch stairs and took his hat off. "All I can say is I'm sorry. I didn't have anything to do with poisoning the trees. Whatever I can do to make things right, I'm goin' to do it."

"Does that mean replanting the acreage you were paid to cut down?" Laura asked.

"I've already given a letter to the county commissioners offering to do that at my own expense," Bentley said, staring back at Laura.

"Come on, William," Sarah said from the buggy. "Let's go on back home."

"Hush!" Bentley said firmly. "You talk too much!" Sarah sat back, wide-eyed and chastised.

His father spoke again. "If you'd take as good care of the land as you do her, everyone would be better off."

Without saying another word, Bentley lifted his wife down from the wagon and looked at Laura. "Mrs. Wilder, do you need another hand inside cleaning my father's house?"

Laura smiled. "Does she know how to clean?"

"No, but it's about time she learned."

"William, I will not clean this house!"

"You will, too. Now get in there and earn your keep for a change!"

Giggling, Laura grabbed Sarah's hand and pulled her toward the door. "Oh, I think we've got a bucket and mop that she can begin with."

Seeing Rev. Youngun, Bentley called out, "Hey, Reverend, think you can put my son to work?"

"With pleasure," Rev. Youngun laughed. Silly Willy got off his horse, grumbling. His father grabbed him by the shirtsleeve.

"And, son."

"Yes, Father?"

"Take off those silly-looking clothes. Reverend Youngun, please find my son a workshirt and old pants from the attic."

Rev. Youngun laughed. "You bet! Come on, Willy. It's time you learned to sweat!"

Bentley grabbed the end of a crosscut saw and motioned Manly to come with him. Stopping before he took the first pull on the saw, Bentley looked Manly in the eye. "I hope to make up for the things I said, Manly."

Manly pulled back the saw. "Just takes time, William— just takes time."

They sawed for a moment; then Bentley stopped. "I need to ask you a favor, Manly."

"What's that?"

"Will you destroy that picture of my wife sittin' in the punch bowl? I don't want Summers to print it in his fool paper."

Manly smiled. "I'll ask Laura to do that, since she's the one that was dancin' with her."

They both laughed, pulling the crosscut saw back and forth.

At dusk, after most of the work was done and the neighbors were packing up to head home, Laura saw William Bentley sitting on a log, staring off toward the sunset.

He picked up a tree seedling and looked at it. "It's funny. This is what you've been trying to show me all along—to take care of the land and replant what we've cut."

"William, money can blind you if you're not careful."

Bentley looked up and smiled. "Sometimes a person can forget what's important. I haven't stopped to look at a sunset —I mean *really* look at a sunset—in years, and I guess I haven't looked inside myself for about as long."

"It's never too late to change," Laura said quietly.

As the two former enemies made peace, the sunset painted the Ozark hills in a splendor of colors and the ever-wondrous sounds of nature sang of night to come.

CHAPTER 37

ALL'S WELL THAT ENDS WELL

A phone was ringing. Laura looked up from her desk. "Please answer it, Manly."

Manly walked into the kitchen and picked up the receiver of the wall phone.

"Hello. No, Rose is not here."

He hung up the phone disgustedly and came into Laura's study. She had just finished up her next column for the *Mansfield Monitor* and signed it boldly.

"Laura, ever since I got you that silly phone, it rings all the time! Why, it's already rung once today!"

Laura smiled. "Manly, you're getting to be an old fuddy-duddy."

"Next thing you'll be wanting is one of those new Sears buggies with automobile seats. That buggy costs $77.45. That's too much!"

When she didn't answer, he added, "Who needs a buggy with automobile seats, anyway?"

Laura looked back at her writing tablet, trying to suppress a smile. "Don't want that."

Manly eyed her suspiciously. "Why not? Thought you said everyone had to have one?"

"You can have your old buggy with automobile seats. I don't want it."

"What do you want?" Manly asked.

"Guess."

Manly stamped his foot. "Oh, not that old game again! Why don't you guess what I want?"

Laura put a finger on her cheek. "Okay. You want a big meal and a hammock so you can lie down and sleep like an old dog."

"Come on, guess."

"Give me a hint," she said playfully.

"Okay. It sounds like this—baaa-baaa."

"We already have sheep," she said, giggling over the silly way he made the sounds.

"I know," Manly smiled. "I want that new Wizard Sheep Shearing Machine that the salesman said would increase our wool profits several times over."

Laura put her pencil down and stared at him.

"But we don't sell much wool to speak of, Manly. We only have a dozen sheep."

The phone rang again, and Manly limped out to answer it, saying, "There's money to be made in sheep, Laura. There's money to be made. The man said so."

Laura whispered to herself, "Selling to Manly is like taking a lamb to slaughter."

"Hey, Laura," Manly called from the kitchen, "Summers wants you to meet him on the east road out of town."

"Did he say why?"

"No, just there was something he wants you to see."

After a short buggy ride with Jack sitting next to her, Laura and Manly came around the bend. Where before the lumber crews had only been clearing the trees, there was a whole crew of Bentley's men planting tree seedlings.

Tears came to her eyes. The land was being reborn.

Laura stepped out of the buggy with the help of Andrew Jackson Summers. "Well, Laura, what do you think? The press is powerful, isn't it?" He took Laura by the shoulders and turned her toward the new sign on the edge of the road.

BENTLEY LAND AND TIMBER COMPANY
APPROVED BY THE AMERICAN FORESTRY ASSOCIATION
(AND LAURA INGALLS WILDER!)

William Bentley stepped from behind the sign, tipping his hat. "You were right when you urged me to replant for the future." He turned to look at the land around them and added, "You're right, Laura. We are the heirs of the ages."

Laura looked over, smiling. "I'm happy for you . . . for all of us. These trees will be a symbol of your caring long after we're gone."

Old Man Bentley hobbled up and stood next to his son, who put his arm around his aging father. The elder Bentley winked at Laura. "And you've shown me the way back to my father," William said.

Old Man Bentley said, "You can worship land, money, and flags, but it all don't mean a hoot—"

"What?" his son asked.

"You didn't let me finish. Like I was about to say, you can worship land, money, and flags, but it all don't mean a hoot unless you've got faith."

Bentley took them on a walking tour to explain his conservation efforts and what he'd planned for the future. After joking with the crew, Manly walked Laura to the top of the hill to survey it all.

Manly put his arm around Laura. "This is exactly what you wanted, Laura Ingalls Wilder—everything you wanted."

Laura smiled slyly and kissed him on the cheek. "Not *everything* I wanted, Manly."

Manly got that worried look on his face. "Now what do you want? Dadgum-it! First you wanted a two-story house, so I built it. Then you wanted the mortgage paid off, so I paid it. Then you wanted water, so I put it in. And then you wanted a telephone, so I . . ."

She cut him off. "No, I earned the money for the telephone by writing for the newspaper."

"Well, that's so, but I'm the one who got you to write for it in the first place, so I figure we're sort of fifty-fifty on the squawk box."

Laura kissed him on the cheek again. "But there's just one more small thing I want, and I know you'll figure a way to get it for me."

Manly dropped his arm. "Oh, Laura, not a . . ."

"Yes."

A few weeks later, Laura drove her new little toboggan-dash Oldsmobile with the dos-à-dos seat into Mansfield. She had read the book on how to drive, and Manly fixed up a circle on the farm for her to practice in. The first week she practiced, the hens stopped laying and the cow's milk all but dried up.

This was her first time behind the wheel on the open road, and she was trying to remember what Manly had taught her about the stick shift, brakes, and clutch. Jack came racing behind her, and Manly was not far behind in the buggy, with Rose screaming, "Stop, Mother! Wait for us!"

Maurice and Eulla Mae jumped out of the way as she came around the bend, and Sheriff Peterson took out his speeding ticket book and started running after her car. The Youngun's dog, Dangit, jumped up on the back of a wagon and began howling.

"A woman—driving!" muttered Maurice. "Imagine that!"

"What're you talkin' 'bout, Maurice? You don't know how to drive a car, either! You never drove a car in your life!"

"Dangit, woman, why you always jumpin' on me?"

Just then Dangit ripped the cuff off Maurice's pants. While Eulla Mae laughed, he kicked the dog away and rubbed his shins.

"That dog is crazy!" Realizing what he said, he backed off. "Dangit, I'm sorry. Gosh dangit, I didn't mean to use your name like that." Dangit came at him again and chased him down the street.

Laura was riding along as if she owned the world. When she waved to Lafayette Bedal, she almost hit the mailbox alongside the road, forcing Rev. Youngun, who was buggy riding again with the widow Carla Pobst, off the road.

Rev. Youngun took off his hat. "Heaven help us—Laura's got a car!"

"I wish you did," Carla said, looking at the buggy.

William Bentley came out onto the front porch of his office, his hands on his hips, laughing. "Maybe I should write an article about safe driving," he shouted.

Larry, Terry, and Sherry raced out to see what all the commotion was and ended up running in front of the car all the way around the block. They saved themselves by jumping into the town pond.

"I thought we were on our way to heaven," Larry said.

"Almost runned over like skunks on the road," muttered Terry.

"It's a miracle we survived," added Larry.

"A miracle!" said Sherry. "Hallelujah!"

As they got out of the water and stood on the edge of the road dripping, Laura came flying around the corner in reverse, sending them back into the pond for safety.

Laura Ingalls Wilder had her car!

About the Author

T.L. Tedrow is a bestselling author, screenwriter, and film producer. His books include the eight-book "Days of Laura Ingalls Wilder Series:" *Missouri Homestead, Children of Promise, Good Neighbors, Home to the Prairie, The World's Fair, Mountain Miracle, The Great Debate,* and *Land of Promise,* which are the basis of a new television series. His four-book series on The Younguns, to be released in 1993, has also been sold as a television series. His first bestseller, *Death at Chappaquiddick,* has been made into a feature film. He lives with his wife, Carla, and four children in Winter Park, Florida.